CINEMA IN AN AGE OF TERROR

FRANCE OVERSEAS:
Studies in Empire and Decolonization

SERIES EDITORS:
Philip Boucher, A. J. B. Johnston, James D. Le Sueur, and Tyler Stovall

Cinema in an Age of Terror

North Africa, Victimization, and Colonial History

MICHAEL F. O'RILEY

University of Nebraska Press
Lincoln and London

Library of Congress Cataloging-
in-Publication Data
O'Riley, Michael F.
Cinema in an age of terror:
North Africa, victimization, and
colonial history / Michael F. O'Riley.
p. cm. — (France overseas)
Includes bibliographical
references and index.
ISBN 978-0-8032-2809-2
(cloth : alk. paper)
1. Motion pictures—Political aspects.
2. Africa, North—In motion pictures.
3. Algeria—History—Revolution,
1954–1962—Motion pictures and the
revolution. 4. Motion pictures—
France—History—20th century.
5. France—In motion pictures.
6. Imperialism in motion pictures.
7. Postcolonialism in motion pictures.
8. East and West in motion pictures.
I. Title. II. Series.
PN1995.9.P6075 2010
791.43'65861—dc22
2009045921

Designed and set in
Galliard by Nathan Putens.

Contents

Acknowledgments

This project began at Ohio State University. I wish to thank my colleague Judith Mayne for her excellent advice and for reading part of the manuscript. Danielle Marx-Scouras, Dana Renga, Gene Holland, and Karlis Racevskis offered their encouragement and support for this project. I would like to thank Jean-Luc DeSalvo and Dominique van Hooff for their kind invitation to present part of this work at San José State University. As always, many thanks to Françoise Calin, Lawrence Busenbark, Henry Garrity, and Jack Yeager for listening.

I have received support from numerous colleagues outside Ohio State University. I wish to thank Barry Sarchet, Leonard Koos, Mary Vogl, and Mimi Mortimer for their conversation and encouragement. The Film Studies program at OSU has been a great resource and a wonderful home. I am grateful to Robert Lount, Steven Oliver, Liz Factor, and Jason Middlemiss in different ways. As always, I wish to thank my parents, Don and Arlene O'Riley.

Introduction

Crumpling trade towers, suicide bombers, burning embassies, and tortured bodies have become commonplace images of what one might term the age of terror. Such images not only highlight the victimization of the perpetrated but also of the author of such acts, the terrorist. These spectacles of victimization raise questions as to what we are to do with such images and what type of response is appropriate. When accompanied by discourses referencing imperialist oppression as an underlying motivation, they also demonstrate the centrality of victimization and imperialist history in terrorist acts that have become commonplace today. The history of Western imperialism, for instance, was noted by terrorists as a key motivation in the World Trade Center attacks. My use of the phrase "the age of terror" is meant to designate a tendency in the post–cold war era of reciprocal forms of terrorism and torture where victimization referencing colonial history functions as a central organizing tenet of national and international relations.[1] While it is beyond the scope of this work to examine all of the various instances of terrorism and torture and the ways they are designated by perpetrators as acts of terror or simply of retribution, it is my objective to elucidate the ways that victimization and imperialist history can be understood to shape violence, occupation, control, and representation between nations and within them. The works examined in this book illustrate how reciprocal forms of violence and territorialism common to larger geopolitical patterns operate, and how many of them go further to demonstrate how victimization and the return of colonial history intricately connect to terror.

What is frequently at stake in spectacles of victimization related to acts of terrorism is the return of a history of imperialist victimization and an attempt to occupy or fully represent the position of victim. If, as Edward Said has argued, imperialism is characterized by territorialist encroachment, a cultural drive to occupy the position of the Other, then we might say that what characterizes the return of imperialist history today is the desire to occupy the position or territory of the victim.[2] In this way, the victim's position is the new space of the age of terror, where the victimized might generate other victims, the terrorized might terrorize, and the terrorized nation state might establish, at a very minimum, the illusion of control through its victimization of other nations. What is at stake is a contest over the space and image of the victim.

In this book I seek to demonstrate how filmic representations of colonial-era victimization can be understood to inform these dynamics. By examining works that represent colonial history and the dynamics of spectatorship that emerge from them, I attempt to demonstrate how the centrality of victimization in certain filmic representations of colonial history can help us understand how the desire to occupy the victim's position — to create a visual spectacle around it — is a dangerous yet blinding drive that frequently plays into the vision of terrorism. I examine how, in some instances, the focus on victimization from the colonial era found in certain films and acts of viewing simply precludes an engagement with concrete problems of the age of terror that the films seek to address. In such cases I examine how the importance accorded to victimization in postcolonial representations of colonial history simply exacerbates cultural tensions. The works examined here all exemplify, in different ways, how a focus on the image of victimization in the representation of colonial history can prove to be a problematic perspective — one that seeks to occupy an ideological territory.[3] In this way, they tell a story about the larger role that victimization and colonial history play today.

Contemporary instances of terror tend to be distilled into Samuel Huntington's famous diagnosis of the "clash of civilizations," opposing the West and Islam. As a catchword "the clash of civilizations" has acquired currency particularly in the wake of September 11. This perspective, replete with the categorization of cultural territory where the West and Islam occupy cultural zones, organizes itself through the very notion of potential victims of a clash.[4] In recent attention to Huntington's formulation, the age of terror becomes identified with the competing claims of victims of terrorist violence.[5] The films examined in this book speak to the vicissitudes of victimization as an organizing principle of representation and cultural claim. Some of them suggest that the claim of victimization and the fascination with it can easily lead to a repetitive cycle whereby the victim and victimizer become one and the same. Others demonstrate how the focus on victimization as a form of resistance is a misleading perspective.

This work emanates from a dearth of critical commentary on the relationship between contemporary incarnations of terrorism after September 11 and their relationship to colonial history. In the wake of September 11, cinema studies has not yet fully interpreted the status of cinematic representation and its relationship to terrorism. Cinema from and about North Africa remains an area that has received little attention despite its contextual relationship to terrorism and victimization. Recently, an upsurge in films focusing on North Africa's colonial history has been witnessed. The argument of this book centers on the ways this colonial history is represented against the contextual backdrop of contemporary terrorism. Given that the colonial history germane to North Africa is often cited by terrorists as an underlying motive for their victimization of the West, it affords a particularly compelling case study. Moreover, the ongoing issues of cultural clash and negotiation emanating from the history of victimization and colonialism shared by North Africa and France provide important commentary on the context of terrorism and its relationship to imperialist history. An examination of some of the most popular international films from and about North Africa offers the opportunity to consider the relationship between victimization, colonial history, visual representations of terror, and terrorism.

Third Cinema, Resistance, and Victimization

Although the films I examine in this book would not all be considered strictly postcolonial by practitioners of postcolonial studies, they all address the status of the postcolonial representation of colonial history in our contemporary context. The works discussed in the following chapters present salient examples of the centrality of victimization in the visual representation of colonial history. More importantly, perhaps, they all provide the opportunity to consider the role of spectatorship in the return of colonial history. One of the central questions to emerge from this consideration is the status of resistance cinema within the age of terror, a relationship overlooked by theorizations of third cinema.

The most concerted effort to theorize the cinema of decolonization or postcolonial resistance cinema has been made in the conception of third cinema, which was first formulated in the late 1960s by the Argentine directors Fernando Solanas and Octavio Gettino.[6] Solanas and Gettino imagined an aggressive cinema of political transformation that perceived of the camera as a weapon in nationalist struggle against Western imperialist ideologies. Characterized by the "long take" and realist aesthetics, third cinema was profoundly concerned with nationalist struggle and revolution. As a form of resistance to Western ideology, third cinema has become known for its representation of colonial victimization. The exemplary case for most discussions of third cinema, for instance, has proven to be Gillo Pontecorvo's 1966 film, *The Battle of Algiers*.[7] Inspired by the Cuban revolution and the works of Frantz Fanon, third cinema was formulated against the conception of Hollywood cinema and conventional aesthetics. For Solanas and Gettino first cinema is a commercial cinema representing the values of the ruling classes. Hollywood cinema or the adoption of Hollywood style constitutes this category. Second cinema, although concerned with the cause of decolonization and the plight of formerly colonized countries and peoples, uses conventional cinematic technique and style. Third cinema, by contrast, was concerned exclusively with resistance through both style and technique.

The controversial Pentagon screening of *The Battle of Algiers* is one example that underscores the relationship of third cinema to the context of new forms of terrorism and hegemony that emerged in the wake of September 11. When the Pentagon screened Pontecorvo's 1966 film in late summer of 2003 as a pedagogical tool in its war on terror, it did so in the interest of understanding better the nature of Arab insurgency. Representing the plight of the colonized Algerian population and of the French colonizer during the Algerian War, Pontecorvo's film underscored the victimization at the heart of anticolonialist struggle. The Pentagon screening of the film was designed as a way for the U.S. government to understand the nature of Arab terrorism in relationship to Western occupation. This was particularly important given the beginning of American occupation in Iraq and the ensuing issues of terrorism it faced.

The irony of the Pentagon screening is that Pontecorvo's work is largely known as a leftist film, particularly as a new-leftist film of the 1960s and that decade of anticolonial struggle. *The Battle of Algiers* has become the emblem of anticolonial struggle and leftist-leaning politics. Viewed as a pedagogical tool for understanding analogous conflicts in Iraq after September 11 by the U.S. government, the film broadened its earlier spectator base to include those political groups not readily identified with either leftist or anticolonial sentiment. The appropriation of the political film in the wake of September 11 raises questions about the return of the resistance film focused on colonial-era victimization in North Africa within the contemporary context. In particular the screening demonstrates how the spectacle of victimization and the victim's position can become appropriated in the name of terrorism. On one hand, the U.S. government's use of *The Battle of Algiers* represented a response to its perceived victimization by an Arab insurgency on September 11. On the other, it also represented a way of viewing the spectacles of victimization represented in the film in order to victimize others in the extension of its hegemony. This return of colonial history from North Africa on screen represents, we might say, a tactics of surveillance of Arab populations elsewhere and an attempt to repress resistance. In a larger sense the dynamics of spectatorship witnessed in the screening of *The Battle of Algiers* suggest the imperative of reevaluating third cinema in the age of terror and its attendant questions of victimization.

Discussion of resistance cinema has, by and large, remained framed by concerted attention to the terms outlined by Solanas and Gettino. Frequently, concern with the dialectical opposition of third cinema to first and second cinema organizes such discussions. Mike Wayne's recent work, *Political Cinema: The Dialectics of Third Cinema*, for instance, is deeply concerned with the theorization of the different categories of cinema and their relationship to one another.[8] Ranjanna Khanna's recent discussion of *The Battle of Algiers* in relationship to the films of Assia Djebar situates the discussion of women's agency in relationship to both third and fourth cinema. For Khanna fourth cinema presents an oppositional term that cuts through the constraints of third cinema and its portrayal of women.[9] Although Khanna admits that her work is less concerned with formulating a theory of resistance than in diagnosing the structural patterns that have led to the elision or inclusion of women in filmic narrative, her diagnosis proceeds through reference to third and fourth cinema and ultimately defines itself through the question of resistance.

Concern with the dialectics of the categories proposed by Solanas and Gettino reflects an ongoing desire to identify a cinema of profound resistance within the contemporary context. Teshome Gabriel's seminal work *Third Cinema in the Third World* encapsulates this desire to identify the potential for "a revolutionary transformation of society" in "films with social relevance and innovative style and, above all, with political and ideological overtones" (4). More recently, postcolonial cinema reflecting issues of cultural hybridity, multiculturalism, and diaspora has been compared to third cinema and, even when distinguished from it, understood to be synonymous with the resistance identified in third cinema. Hamid Naficy's discussion of North African films and cultural hybridity as an example of an "accented cinema" that shares the qualities of cinema *engagé* is perhaps the most important example of the way third cinema has become associated with other forms of postcolonial resistance cinema (31).[10]

My objective in evoking the debates surrounding third cinema and its variations is not to engage specifically with the terms of that debate, but rather to point out that what seems to be missing in the debate surrounding resistance and the representation of colonial history and its aftermath in cinema is an engagement with the context of terrorism. Even the recent volume *Rethinking Third Cinema*, which sets out to reconsider the status of third cinema in the contemporary context, makes no mention of the relationship of third cinema, or postcolonial cinema, to terrorism or the age of terror. Most works treating the status of postcolonial cinema, like those mentioned above, exhibit a policing of its terms, or an insistent attention to categorizations of resistance, in their concern with third cinema. What is most compelling in this attention to the resistant qualities of the terms of a cinema of decolonization is the critical fascination that still prevails with identifying resistance in films treating, by and large, the 1960s and that era's history of colonial resistance. Such attention raises a number of questions, some of which are evident in the Pentagon screening of *The Battle of Algiers*. First, do the issues raised by resistance films and the portrayal of victimization from earlier periods of colonial history still hold relevance today in relation to neoimperialist issues? How might imperialist ideologies screen those portrayals of victimization and appropriate the very category of victim for their own uses to define the age of terror? What does the critical focus on colonial-era victimization in third cinema suggest about the ability of the critical response to confront the contemporary context? In other words, does a focus on the representation of colonial-era history as a political antidote suggest an incapacitated critical response with respect to the contemporary context? Lastly, does the victimization found in representations of colonial history present a dangerous ideology in the contemporary context?

In this book my concern is not to engage specifically with what constitutes resistance cinema or in a reevaluation of the aesthetic categories of third cinema. Rather, I am interested in what the return of colonial history and a focus on victimization within it in cinema from and about North Africa might mean within the contemporary context. I am concerned primarily with how returns of colonial history, such as those witnessed in the screening of *The Battle of Algiers*, inform the role of victimization in the representation of colonial history in our contemporary context. The films examined in this book and the dynamics of spectatorship they engage raise the question of whether the debate about resistance surrounding the representation of colonial history is still relevant given the nature of reciprocal victimization witnessed in recent manifestations of terror. In other words they ask whether the return of colonial history and victimization on screen might still constitute a form of resistance within the contemporary context.

Postcolonial Theory and the Return of Colonial History

The visual representation of victimization and the return of colonial history in North Africa occupy a significant position in the theorization of postcolonial resistance. An important strain of postcolonial theory treating the representation of colonial history is implicitly built upon the visualization of victimization. Interestingly, North

Africa proves to be a privileged site for these dynamics in postcolonial theory. In many postcolonial films treating North Africa, as in many postcolonial theories that reference the North African context, a focus on projecting or viewing the victim from colonial history is central. Frequently, such representations of the victim are conceived as a way of formulating resistance or effecting transformation for minorities. At worst, the focus on the victim's position, or the return of the spectacle of victimization suffered in the past, mirrors the ideological contest over the control of victimization we see in the age of terror. This is perhaps best exemplified in the way the Pentagon screening of *The Battle of Algiers* was very much about understanding and controlling the perceived threat of victimization to the United States identified in the film while simultaneously using that information as a way of thinking about the U.S. occupation — or victimization — of Iraq. However, at best, the focus on colonial-era victimization in these returns of colonial history often proves to be severed from the contemporary context they seek to transform.

Rachid Bouchareb's award-winning film *Days of Glory*, or *Indigènes*, is one example of a postcolonial film that seeks to return the history of colonization to the former colonizer. Focusing on North African colonized troops that served for France during World War II, Bouchareb's film attempted to bring the victimization that these colonized soldiers faced both during and after their service to the attention of the wider public. Moreover, screened shortly after the 2005 riots in France that found youths of Maghrebian heritage disenfranchised, the film sought to speak to a younger generation of Maghrebian youths. Indeed, the film did attract the attention of France's president Jacques Chirac. After screening the film Chirac agreed to raise the frozen pensions of the North African soldiers who fought for France and bring them in line with those of the French soldiers. However, this gesture seemed to have little to do with the youths of Maghrebian heritage or with the larger forms of repression and terror witnessed during the 2005 riots — and earlier versions of them — by the French government, namely the imposition of sovereign law dating to the colonial era.[11] Such repression was also a part of a larger geopolitical conception of the division of the West and its Arab other, and was widely viewed as a fitting example of the "clash of civilizations."

I evoke Bouchareb's film here to demonstrate how the return of images of colonial-era victimization can at times be disconnected from the contemporary context of terror. While Bouchareb's film was clearly successful in motivating Chirac, it is unclear to what degree Chirac's acknowledgement of colonial history proved a simple gesture with little relevance to the contemporary issues of terror affecting citizens of North African heritage and origin in France. Like Bouchareb's film, a good deal of postcolonial theory concerned with the projection of the image of colonial-era victimization proves questionable within the contemporary age of terror. Postcolonial theory, like the films I examine in this book, often focuses on imagining or projecting the dramatic spectacle of the colonial-era victim's plight in relation to the colonizer.[12] In this way, a spectacle of the historical victim's return takes precedence in the images of history presented.

Perhaps the most famous return of the victimizing gesture of colonial history in North Africa can be found in Malek Alloula's examination of the Franco-Algerian postcard in *The Colonial Harem*. Like Bouchareb's film, Alloula's project is concerned with demonstrating the way the formerly colonized were victimized by the European colonizer. Like Bouchareb, Alloula is concerned with forcing the former colonizer to view its former subjects differently. Indexing the objectification of Algerian women through the obsessive gaze of the colonizer and the colonial postcard, Alloula's book seeks to "return this immense postcard to its sender" as a form of postcolonial resistance (5). Alloula's project seeks to return the gaze of the victimized nation of Algeria back onto the colonizer in an act of postcolonial defiance and representative agency. However, colonial history and its victimization in Algeria are returned not only to the sender in Alloula's work, but also to the contemporary age of terror. Certainly, Alloula's work has the quality of an archive of one aspect of colonial history that is easily forgotten. However, as a work that is still widely read in the contemporary context, *The Colonial Harem* raises the question of how and whether the type of colonial-era victimization represented and returned by Alloula's work is still relevant to the contemporary context.[13] Moreover, the gesture of defiance and victimization explicit in the work raises the question about whether the "clash of civilizations" between the West and its Other that has in many ways come to characterize the contemporary context does not upstage the work's revisionist qualities. The focus in Alloula's work becomes that of positioning or reversing the victim and victimizer positions to align with a division between the West and its Other. Although Alloula's work constitutes an attempt to expose the dynamics of the representation of colonial history, it is also a gesture organized around the victimizing position. My point here is not to align Alloula's postcolonial act of revisionist history with terrorist ideology, but rather to point out how works of postcolonial defiance focusing on colonial-era victimization frequently mirror divisions and cultural tensions that have come to define the age of terror. The question then becomes how we might view these works and the dynamics of spectatorship they engender as relevant forms of resistance within the contemporary context. Might it be better to view works such as *The Colonial Harem* as diagnostic tools for the dynamics of victimization rather than as defiant and resistant models for the contemporary context? Is the lesson to be learned from them not that the spectacle of victimization of colonial history remains central to divisions we see in the age of terror? Does a focus on victimization and divisions between a "Western" colonizer and the colonized that we see in postcolonial representations reproduce and exacerbate ideological divisions that often characterize terrorism today?

The fascination with the visual spectacle of colonial violence and victimization with respect to North Africa and, in particular, Algeria is common in much postcolonial criticism. Like Alloula, Robert Young is interested in the way the image of colonial-era victimization might serve as resistance within the contemporary context. In *Postcolonialism: An Historical Introduction* Young attempts to rethink political determination through a privileging of the anticolonial liberation struggles of North Africa.[14] At the same time, however, Young's evocation of victimization in his discussion of the Algerian War fascinates the critical gaze with images of the colonial spectacle of violence, ultimately leading to a fixation with the colonial era that makes it difficult to see its relationship to the conditions of the age of terror he would like to resist. Young's interpretation of the images of colonial history demonstrates how the return of colonial history often focuses on victimization with little reflection on how that category and its contest contribute to contemporary tensions that, in part, produce the age of terror. I place particular emphasis here on the returning or projected images of victimization from colonial history as they relate to the contemporary context, because the films I examine in this work all raise the question of how we might see the relationship of colonial-era victimization to the present.

Young begins with an evocation of photos he claims disturbed him during the writing of the book and which provide a salient embodiment of the postcolonial according to him (ix).[15] The first photo, titled "Les porteuses de bombes des stades: l'âge de Juliette, l'âme de Ravachol" (Stadium Bomb Carriers: The Age of Juliette, the Soul of Ravachol), presumably shows Djouher Akhor and Baya Hocine, the young unveiled Algerian women who were arrested for placing bombs in the Algiers and El-Biar stadiums on 10 February 1957 and whose history interested Simone de Beauvoir. Young's particular identification with victimization from colonial-era conflict in the photographic image obfuscates contemporary resistance and further removes his critique from the contemporary context.

In the intense gaze of the close-up shot of the two young women, Young distinguishes "a slightly sensual aura," a defiance that will turn the victimized women into victimizers (viii). The tension of this aura, found in the "defiant eyes" and "slightly parted" lips of one of the young women, is conflated with a solemn, if unveiled, sexuality when Young characterizes the emancipatory nature of the photo as "Algeria unveiled indeed" (viii).[16] The distancing of Young's criticism by the conflation of the visual memento of victimization and fantasy of colonial-era sexuality and phallic dynamics is only reinforced by his evocation of a second photo, this time featuring a scene he identifies as homoerotic.

Young describes a "nature morte" depiction of four European men holding up a naked man, "clearly an Algerian," as if "giving him the bumps, the homoerotic play of sportsmen" (ix). Here, Young detects the anxiety of the terrorized Algerian, whose exposed genitals evoke "a contorted 'spread shot' in a pornographic magazine," in the man's look of "abject fear, misery, and terror" (ix). The rather bizarre reference to homoeroticism here seems placed gratuitously to imbue the scene with the anxiety of a more historically situated, contemporary form of cultural conflict: "What were the colons about to do to him, as he was posed for the photograph, poised between life and death?" (ix). While it is difficult to imagine what is homoerotic in a scene of "abject fear, misery, and terror" defined by colonial struggle, it is clear that Young turns to the anxiety within the struggles of rape and seduction that permeate colonial space through reference to the affective dimensions of both homosexual and heterosexual psychic life. These colonial sites of victimization become an ideological space, according to Young, from which the ideals of postcolonial resistance might be derived. I evoke Young's engagement with the visualization of victimization from the archive of colonial history to suggest how the spectatorship of colonial scenes of victimization can become invested in the desire to identify resistance to contemporary conditions of terror. Such desires, focused as they are on the victimizing impulse in colonial history, frequently signal an abyss between the represented images of colonial history and the contemporary context of viewing.[17] Like many of the films and their receptions examined in this work, Young's focus on and, one might say, imagination of the spectacle of victimization establish a questionable relationship between colonial history and the contemporary context of viewing.

In a similar manner, Iain Chambers focuses on the return of colonial history that might give rise to a questioning of contemporary forms of oppression while ultimately overlooking contemporary contexts. Chambers's attempt to visualize and situate the remnants of colonial history in North Africa within the European metropolis represents a broader postcolonial emphasis on the visual mapping of colonial history — an attempt to visually locate the traces of colonial history on the European cultural map. Like Bouchareb in *Days of Glory*, Chambers is concerned with situating and mapping colonial history within Europe as a mode of resistance. Although this mapping process is designed to awaken consciousness of colonial history, it is based on the concept of returning victimization and an ensuing division between the West and its Arab other.

Chambers turns to postcolonial France and its legacy of Arab immigration to illustrate the concept of the return of colonial history as a disruptive presence capable of transforming the Western consciousness into a victim-witness of its own history. Referring to an Arab scribe with a portable desk, wrapped in a *djellaba* and wearing a turban, Chambers claims that he can discern a disruptive presence in the history of colonial subjugation that the image provides (*Culture* 206). Chambers says that this encounter embodies a limit for occidental consciousness as it is haunted by the Arab and the history of colonialism and its failure that he represents: "The Arab scribe as referent of my discourse both unfolds towards me and away from me, is both object of my narrative and a subject in a world that is never simply mine" (206). In this situated encounter Chambers focuses on a form of postcolonial "anxiety" that comes from the encounter with colonial history, the return of the colonial repressed in the form of the Freudian *unheimlich*, or unhomely (207). This scene that "exceeds immediate understanding" for the Western witness, according to Chambers, provides an example of how the return of colonial history is frequently constructed as a haunting or victimizing spectacle (207).[18] Here, the spectacle of the return of colonial history is based upon an artificially constructed divide between the West and a removed Arab world. Indeed, it is difficult to see precisely what is "interruptive" in this normal encounter. Moreover, Chambers' example is representative of the way the visualization of North African colonial history often serves as the basis for theories of resistance while remaining severed from the contemporary context. How, for instance, does the colonial history of North Africa relate to the contemporary context Chambers is addressing? What is the nature of the relationship between the Arab scribe and forms of globalization, for instance, as he waits, as Chambers tells us, for illiterate clients — immigrants from the Maghreb and elsewhere — to pay him a meager sum to write letters in Arabic? What is the relationship between the French colonial legacy and the contemporary forms of oppression experienced by Maghrebian immigrants?

In attempting to situate North African colonial history within the European metropolis, Chambers attempts to return colonial history to the European center, much like Malek Alloula. This return, not unlike the cinematic portrayal of colonial history on screen, functions as an attempt to inscribe or map colonial history as a visually victimizing presence within the contemporary context.

Like Alloula, Chambers, and Young, Homi Bhabha turns to the concept of the visual projection of colonial-era images of victimization as a way of placing the victims of colonial history on the European map. Rachid Bouchareb's *Indigènes*, much like these postcolonial theories concerning the returning images of colonial history, is also structured by the cartographic process of placing victims on the European map. As the North African soldiers' campaign moves from North Africa through the regions of France to the north, aerial maps serve as narrative devices that tell the larger story of the soldiers' sacrifice and victimization. The maps not only locate the movement of the soldiers' campaign but also serve to symbolically situate the history of their colonial victimization within France. Bouchareb demonstrates, like Bhabha and other postcolonial theorists, a keen interest in projecting the occluded history of colonialism and its victims within the heart of European consciousness through the mapping process.

Bhabha's conception of a "belated" return of colonial history as a visual map of victimization is rooted, much like that of the films examined in this book, in the colonial history of victimization in North Africa. Much of Bhabha's theory of the belated return of colonial history can be traced to his engagement with what he calls "scenes" of oppression located in the work of Frantz Fanon and his discussion of colonial history in North Africa. A scene of Fanon's *Black Skin, White Masks* describing how a Negro is subjected to racist terms serves as a recurring scene in Bhabha's work from which he devises the notion of a haunting colonial temporality, what he identifies as "the belatedness of the black man" (*Location* 236). Bhabha argues that Fanon's repetition of the scene/seen of oppression serves as a point of identification through which the colonial past and its scenes of oppression are reiterated and projected into modernity as a means of questioning "the ontology of man" (238). This belated return of colonial history, according to Bhabha, revises the very dynamics of the black man's subjection and of the white man's supremacy.

According to Bhabha the belated temporality of colonial history and its repressed subjects is an essentially disruptive force. Bhabha thus draws upon what he calls the "memorial map" of "Slavery, War, Holocaust, migration, diaspora" as histories that might counter contemporary experiences of transnational culture that create inequalities ("World" 203). The colonial past is "repeated" or "projected" in the present and therefore disrupts "the continuum of history" (*Location* 254, 257). This disruption is based upon a mapping process that attempts to visually project colonial history and its attendant questions of victimization into the present. What remains central to this belated return of colonial history, we might say, is the territory of the victim or the spectacle of the victim's claim to space and territory within the contemporary context. My claim in this book is that the spectacle of victimization we see in many films about North Africa is problematic because it ultimately reveals an ideological contest over the territory of the victim — a contest to occupy the victim's position or to control the territory that we frequently see displayed in the spectacular events of terror within our contemporary context.

Cartographies of Victimization

The intersection of history, visual plotting, and ideology has recently been identified in cinema as a mapping process. Tom Conley's formulation of cinema as a cartographic process that maps or situates history and the imaginary of the spectator is similar to the cartographic processes implicit in postcolonial theories of the return of colonial history and its victimization. For Conley a film can be understood in a broad sense to be a map "that plots and colonizes the imagination of the public it is said to invent and, as a result, to seek to control" (1). A film, like a topographic projection, is an image that incites the viewer to see the world in relation to its own conception of space and being. Implicit in Conley's conception of cinema as a cartographic process is an underlying conception of victimization. The projected image acts upon the viewer and space in a contest to occupy ideological territory or "to victimize" the spectator.[19] In a similar manner, the postcolonial conception of the return of colonial history, as I have outlined above, is frequently based upon the projected image of victimization and its control over the ideological position or territory of the victim. What is imperative is the process of putting colonial history on the map.

The returns of colonial history examined in this book all engage with the creation of what we might call cartographies of victimization. The representations of colonial history and its aftermath that they portray all engage with what it means to "map" the history of colonial victimization within the age of terror. Although all of the films and the issues of spectatorship examined in this work don't necessarily include literal maps showing victims, they do raise the question of what it means to project colonial history as a history of victimization within the present. In this sense, they all raise the fundamental question of the ideological consequences of the return of victimization as a central organizing structure. As such, they underscore how the desire to control the projection or representation of victimization remains at the heart of the representation of colonial history.

It is not surprising that North Africa plays a central role in postcolonial discussions of victimization and colonial history. The desire to imagine or map colonial history from North Africa is understandable. The extended history of French imperialism in Algeria, Morocco, and Tunisia has created an intermingling of Western and indigenous cultures. That mixture of cultures and the tensions it has produced have proven particularly difficult for Algeria and Tunisia to realize the promises of independence from the colonial power that were implicit in the decolonization movement — namely, democracy and peaceful coexistence of populations. The centrality of the Algerian War as a point of reference for the struggle between the West and colonized Algerians is an important explanation for a great deal of the postcolonial interest in North Africa; it served as a defining moment for North Africa and for the Western imaginary that sympathized with the decolonization movement.[20]

The reason for my focus on North Africa in this book is based in part on the prevailing tensions of colonial history found in the area. It is also based on the fact that North Africa remains a region where larger issues of the age of terror are reflected through the projection or insistence of that colonial history. The confrontation of Western ideals and more extremist versions of Islamic fundamentalism, particularly in Algeria, has produced a civil war replete with terrorist attacks, suicide bombers, and executions. In many ways this situation has simply reproduced the anticolonialist framework of the 1960's independence struggle that opposed the French to North Africans. In this case, though, the conflict is filtered through the opposition of the West and Islamic fundamentalism, an opposition that has come to structure the conception of the age of terror. Most importantly, perhaps, oppositions related to culture, history, and territory that one finds in North Africa are also emblematic of larger patterns.

The spectacles of victimization that result from such oppositions raise the question of the specter of colonial history. In focusing on films from and about North Africa, this book seeks to explore the larger role that the focus on victimization from colonial history plays in terror. The films I examine all demonstrate how the return and insistence on victimization from colonial history can align with the ideological divisions of the age of terror. These divisions between the West and an Arab world are based upon the image of victimization and the desire to appropriate that image as witnessed in the Pentagon screening of *The Battle of Algiers*. The films I examine speak to our understanding of the contemporary geopolitical context because they demonstrate how victimization remains at the center of a neocolonial dynamics of terrorism that divides the world into Manichean spheres.

This book could be considered a compilation of reflections on the process of mapping colonial-era victimization — its returns, appropriations, and spectacles — in the age of terror. In the first two chapters I consider, respectively, the role of victimization in the returns of colonial history in Pontecorvo's *The Battle of Algiers* and in Bouchareb's *Days of Glory*. In the first chapter I examine how films like *The Battle of Algiers* are viewed as being subversive in relation to the "age of terror" as a way of reformulating notions of third cinema after September 11. This chapter explores how postcolonial resistance cinema becomes appropriated and what the appropriation of visual scenes of victimization from colonial history implies for terrorism and its responses. In the second chapter I explore how Bouchareb's attempt to bring the history of North African soldiers who fought for France to the attention of the public functions in the context of the widespread terrorism and riots that France experienced in 2005. This chapter tackles the political stakes of the representation of colonial history and its relationship to what was termed the "clash of civilizations" in France. In the third chapter I examine Michael Haneke's film *Hidden*, or *Caché*. The film demonstrates how Algeria and its former colonizer remain haunted by the colonial era, victims of the intransigent hold of a colonial past that remains invisible, yet continues to structure cultural memory today. Haneke's film ultimately demonstrates that the desire to view and retrace the history of colonial victimization is symptomatic of the postcolonial inability to see outside the recurring paradigm of victimization from colonial history. Chapter 4 explores how the popular cinema of Maghrebian filmmakers of North African heritage, such as Yamina Benguigui, Soraya Nini, Azouz Begag, and Merzak Allouache, represents the Maghreb in relationship to the process of "Arab" cultural integration in the West. In this chapter I demonstrate how victimization is frequently integral to the establishment of an East-West polarity in films that portray the immigrant legacy of colonial history. I examine how different filmmakers treat the question of the "clash of civilizations" and argue that its representation within the context of terrorism today is a problematic move. My objective in re-reading these popular films in this way is to examine the stakes of their focus on victimization and cultural integration projected within the contemporary context. A comparison of these works demonstrates that the refusal of the victim's posture is central to arresting the cycle of victimization in the age of terror. In chapter 5 the work of Algeria's award-winning author and filmmaker Assia Djebar is of central concern. In that chapter I examine how Djebar's turn to Julien Duvivier's famous colonial-era film, *Pépé le Moko*, serves as the basis for commentary on the pervasiveness of the victim's attitude in North Africa. Djebar's work explores how the inability to see outside the victim's paradigm established by the French colonial presence has perpetuated a bloody cycle of victimization in North Africa. Through an interpretation of Djebar's use of Duvivier's colonial film, I show how the filmmaker addresses the politics of fundamentalism in Algeria and identifies the role that colonial history plays in terrorism today. Djebar's rewriting of Duvivier opens the door to the interplay of history and the contemporary world as well as to a rupture in the cycle of victimization.

The works examined in this book all accommodate the spectacle of victimization from colonial history. Their return of colonial history to our contemporary context, although frequently problematic, enables us to see how victimization is very much about territory — cultural, spatial, and ideological. In so doing they demonstrate that the nature of resistance to new forms of imperialist warfare and terror today must be located outside the haunting images of victimization from colonial history. Such images ultimately only return as spectacular acts that draw our attention away from the cyclical contest over territory that they embody. This said, those images of victimization shall have the last word.

1

Resuscitating *The Battle of Algiers*

The Politics of Race in the War on Iraq

In late summer of 2003, when resistance to the American occupation in Iraq acquired the profile of a war of guerilla insurgency through increased bombings and acts of sabotage, the office of Special Operations and Low-Intensity Conflict at the Pentagon designed and distributed e-mail flyers for those involved in "WOT," or war on terror. The e-mail with the cautionary heading "How to win a battle against terrorism and lose the war of ideas" was an invitation to a special screening of the 1966 masterpiece film *The Battle of Algiers*, by the Italian Marxist director Gillo Pontecorvo.[1] Based on the book *Souvenirs de la bataille d'Algers*, by Saadi Yacef, former leading figure of the FLN (Algerian Nationalist Liberation Front) up until his arrest in 1957, Pontecorvo's film opens on 7 October 1957 as an Algerian nationalist is tortured at the hands of the French Colonel Matthieu. Of course Yacef, who not only served as producer of the film but also starred in it as El-hadi Jaffar, leader of the FLN, acts out events of the battle that led to his own arrest. After the opening scenes of torture, the film returns us to the beginning of the Battle of Algiers on 1 November 1954 to follow the three-year war. A political epic that employs no real documentary footage, the film depicts the conflict between Algerian nationalist insurgents and French colonial forces in the late 1950s (1954–57 to be precise). It is perhaps of interest to point out that the French government referred to this conflict, until as recently as 1999, as the "events," before finally admitting the struggle into official historical record as the Algerian War.

The U.S. Pentagon, too, was not immune to such deformations of colonial history, particularly in its description of the battle for independence from the colonizer in language that focused on Arab terrorism: "Children shoot soldiers at point-blank range. Women plant bombs in cafés. Soon the entire Arab population builds to a mad fervor. Sound familiar?" (U.S. Pentagon flier). Given a few inaccuracies suggestive more of governmental fantasies that superimpose the situation in Iraq and the situation in Algeria (children actually shoot a police officer, and the Algerian population builds more to a sullen withdrawal than to a fervored engagement), the Pentagon identified with the material in Pontecorvo's film as if it were derived from documentary footage.[2] In a *New York Times* article in 2003, Michael Kaufman wrote of a Pentagon screening where "forty officers and civilian experts were urged to consider and discuss the important issues at the core of the film . . . the problematic but alluring efficacy of brutal and repressive means in fighting clandestine terrorists in places like Algeria and Iraq. Or more specifically, the advantages and costs of resorting to torture and intimidation in seeking vital human intelligence about enemy plans." Such identifications were also suggested by former national security advisor Zbigniew Brzezinski, who stated, "If you want to understand what's happening right now in Iraq, I recommend the *Battle of Algiers*."[3]

Of course the U.S. government was not the only party interested in Pontecorvo's classic, although it undoubtedly contributed in great measure to popular interest. The film has recently benefited from release in an enhanced DVD format from the Criterion Collection replete with documentary and interviews, and from ongoing runs at the New York Film Forum, as well as movie houses in Washington, Chicago, LA, and San Francisco. In addition the film has been subject to a slew of reviews and reports in major newspapers and magazines in the United States and Europe. The understandable paradox of such identifications remains that the film is largely known as a film related to the anticolonial struggle. Like films such as Bernardo Bertolucci's *Il Conformista* (The Conformist) and Liliana Cavani's *Il Portiere di notte* (The Night Porter), Pontecorvo's *The Battle of Algiers* participates in the 1960's and 1970's Italian cinematic tradition of revising fascist oppression and depicting criminality as an ambiguous category. Associated with the Algerian War of Independence, the Cuban revolution, Vietnam, the Black Panthers' resistance movement, and, more recently, with the training of troops in Northern Ireland in their struggle with the British, Pontecorvo's film has become the emblem of anticolonial struggle and leftist-leaning politics.[4] The film, like others of its type by filmmakers such as Ousmane Sembene, Alain Resnais, and René Vautier, was banned in France for fear that its politically charged content would incite rebel immigrants or their sympathizers. Viewed as a pedagogical tool for understanding analogous conflicts in Iraq after September 11, the film broadened its earlier spectator base to include those political groups not readily identified with either leftist or anticolonial sentiment.

In this chapter I want to begin by examining the nature of those cinematic identifications. I will explore how, specifically, in reportage surrounding the new release of the film, the turn to discourses of racial identification as a tactic of recognizance and surveillance was made popular. Many of the critical commentaries published after September 11 in the wake of the film's newfound popularity, even when critical of the Pentagon's use of the film in its war on Iraq, evoke discourses rooted in an Orientalist tradition, referencing notions of a history of pan-Arab terrorism in opposition to the West and conjuring "Arabness" as a quasi-racial category. The racial coding found in such reportage in the West aligns largely with the anti-Arab climate related to terrorism in the wake of September 11. I will argue that ultimately this way of viewing the film and "Arabs" in it resonates not only with the larger political climate but also with a larger strategy of Western neoimperialist surveillance and territorial expansion.

This type of Western surveillance, rooted in an Orientalist tradition of identifying and designating an Eastern "Other," was part of a mapping process intended to enable the United States to approach more easily a territory as seemingly alien and forbidding to the U.S. government's mission as it was inviting. Ultimately, this process revealed the ongoing relevance of colonial-era practices in the targeting of foreign and, more precisely, Arab populations and territories for Western occupation. Most importantly, highlighting the centrality of "resistance cinema" to the age of terrorism in the way it did, this process suggested the ways that oppositional or third cinema were dealt debilitating blows.

What these processes underscored was the ongoing history of the Mediterranean as what Iain Chambers has called an "imaginatively constructed" zone of transit (*Mediterranean* 10). For Chambers this type of construction is rooted in a long history of Western imperialist imposition in the Mediterranean, one where the European imagination of the Mediterranean shaped colonial tactics and history, and transformed the Mediterranean space into a subaltern zone. The use of Pontecorvo's film as a historical text from which the narrative of colonial resistance could be reimagined by the Western purview and cast as the threat of Arab insurgency signals the ways that the history of the Mediterranean is still constructed through the optic of imperialism as a space to be surveyed and racially codified as a victimizing presence. As Chambers points out, one of the Mediterranean's principal characteristics is the way it has been subject to a "systematic imperial control of territory" (*Mediterranean* 144). The use of Pontecorvo's film as a pedagogical tool for the imposition of the United States in Iraq suggests how the Mediterranean and, more specifically, Algeria continue to be viewed as a space not only subject to imperialist vision but also as a space from which the West could expand its control of territory. This neoimperialist vision transforms the Marxist aesthetics of Pontecorvo's third cinema into victimizing images identified as a threat to Western hegemony. Ultimately, this way of viewing the resistance of the West and casting the colonial victimization of the Mediterranean as a Western right demonstrates how the texts of postcolonial resistance can be easily appropriated by new incarnations of contemporary imperialism today. What is central to those forms is the colonial mission's drive to possess, which becomes the impetus to appropriate the category of victim through a racial designation and occlusion of colonial history followed by the imposition of tactics of territorial control.

In order to explore this phenomenon, I will examine how reception of the film and commentary on cinematic identification by the film's important critics play in stark contrast to the U.S. understanding and appropriation of victimization in the film. Whether it be the ambiguous treatment of victim and victimizer, or a more overtly oppositional style, its cinematic identification clearly focuses on Muslim terrorism and not on the perception that victim and victimizer are melded in war. The Western process of designating and appropriating victimization evident in the recent screening of *The Battle of Algiers* remains at the center of the dilemma for resistance cinema in the age of terror.

A great deal of recent interest in *The Battle of Algiers* by American spectators as well as by a U.S. government wary of long-term cohabitation with an "Arab" population is based on the perceived reality of the revolutionary nature of Arab terrorism informed by historically received images of Arabs and pan-Arab stereotypes. Despite important contextual differences between the occupation of Algeria and the occupation of Iraq, much reportage linking the two wars draws strict parallels between *The Battle of Algiers* and the current War on Iraq primarily through recourse to race and racially coded images of terrorism and revolution. Strictly speaking, the category of Arab does not constitute a racial designation in conventional terms. However, in reportage either seeking to draw or denounce parallels between *The Battle of Algiers* and the war in Iraq, notions of race and racially coded images of terrorism were evoked, often in surreptitious ways. Frequently, these emerged in the notion of pan-Arab terrorism and in the reliance upon preexisting racial stereotypes played out in reference to both the film and the context of the war in Iraq.

Before turning to some specific examples of these manifestations, I would like to point very briefly to the structural framework that underpins the types of racial and racially coded identifications made in many discussions of parallels between the film and the war on Iraq. Such identification problems can be viewed best, perhaps, in Robert Stam and Louis Spence's report on the film in a recent article on the politics of cinematic identification. Stam and Spence argue that the film constitutes a revolutionary breakthrough, in that it creates conscious political sympathy with the Algerian people. They argue, for instance, that through scale and point-of-view editing, the spectator comes to identify with the struggle of Algerian women planting bombs in cafés, to the point where "the film makes us want the women to complete their task" (29). While Stam and Spence acknowledge the many close-up shots of innocent victims, they argue that "spectatorial positioning is so complete" as to derail any ambiguity concerning the film's message: "Pontecorvo thus hijacks the apparatus of objectivity and the formulaic techniques of mass media reportage . . . to express political views usually anathema to the dominant media. For the First World mass media, terrorism means only freelance or infrastate violence . . . But *Battle of Algiers* presents anticolonialist terror as a response to colonialist violence" (30).[5] While it is easy to agree with Stam and Spence that cinematic identification does take place through spectatorial positioning, such identifications as seen in reportage about the film (particularly from the Pentagon) seem to take place as identifications with Algerians as enemies. Such a positioning propagates the "clash of civilizations," establishing an identification directly related to the conflict in Iraq as Western world versus Arab, or Orient. It is ultimately this specular relationship between West and East that structures the racialized identifications one finds in many commentaries on the film.

One of the first things to note in the Pentagon's viewing of the film as documentary is the biased, indeed exclusive, focus on Arab terrorism and the way it builds. In those discourses there is a complete and utter spectatorial identification with Algerians as an enemy under surveillance. There is no mention whatsoever of Western occupation as terrorism — a point made in the *Battle of Algiers* most explicitly by a captured official of the FLN. Identifications with Algerians, indeed with "Arabs," as terrorists within the context of colonial struggle is perhaps most evident in the documentary case study, which is included with the newly released version of the film. The conversation between Richard Clarke, former national counterterrorism coordinator, and Michael Sheehan, former State Department coordinator for counterterrorism, proceeds through tension between disavowal of Western (American and French) terrorist tactics and occupation, and evocation of the terrorism of the Arab world rooted in a long history. Speaking of "Arab extremism," Sheehan argues that "there is nothing new going on in Iraq that hasn't gone on for over three thousand years." In this respect, it is important to note that this conversation is framed by alternating clips from Pontecorvo's film of veiled and armed Algerians performing acts of what Sheehan and Clarke term "urban terrorism," whereas no images of French colonial activity are featured.

Such notions of pan-Arab terrorism are also evident in reports by journalists who find little historically comparable between Algeria and Iraq. In his *New Yorker* article titled "Winning and Losing," Philip Gourevitch points out the French defeat in the film and states that what does unite the two situations is "the ugly truth" that "terrorism works." Of course the ongoing situation of civil war and unrest in Algeria demonstrates that the Algerians did not necessarily win, a point which seems to illustrate more clearly that terrorism, no matter how defined, does not work.[6] Like Gourevitch, Charles Paul Freund, senior editor of *Reason* magazine, suggests a common revolutionary Arab terrorism in both Algeria and Iraq. In his article titled "The Pentagon's Film Festival: A Primer for *The Battle of Algiers*," Freund concludes that although the two situations are radically different, the "Mideast learned the efficacy of insurgent terror from Algeria. The PLO, Hamas, and other [Arab] groups are indebted to the Algerian strategy. Its lessons are now apparent in Iraq too." Identifications such as these of a pan-Arab terrorism originating in Algeria suggest a disavowal of Western terrorism in the form of colonial invasion and occupation, not to mention the practices of French torture clearly depicted in Pontecorvo's film. To characterize common Algerian and Iraqi resistance to Western occupation in their own countries as terrorism is to posit a Western proprietary right to colonial territory, as if Algerian and Iraqi citizens were never there before Western arrival. As Achille Mbembe reminds us in his work *On the Postcolony*, this is a common trope of colonial discourse that abrogates ownership and cancels or completely disavows "native" settler identity (183).

Moreover, the nature of such pan-Arab terrorism is coded in Orientalist terms as a specific stereotypical address and Western approach to the "East." Although Edward Said associates Orientalism more specifically with the era of active European colonialism, in his more recent work, *Culture and Imperialism*, he notes that American ascendancy into a new imperialist relationship with the world continues the Orientalist lineage in ways that are often controlled by mass media and the culture of the image. For Said, then, contemporary Western media representations of the Arab world frequently exhibit an Orientalist approach "effective in representing strange and threatening foreign cultures for the home audience" (292). Moreover, as Chambers recalls, the colonial tropes of "framing, objectifying, and alienating the 'native'" common in the Mediterranean, have become the tenets of a "universal modernity" now maintained by a Western approach that continues to define itself against an Other and thereby maintain "planetary order" (*Mediterranean* 7). The interviews included with the new release of Pontecorvo's film display just such an Orientalist representation of the Mediterranean. The conversation between Clarke and Sheehan focuses, as does the Pentagon's statement about the film, on the "mad fervor" of "Arabs." Nonetheless, for Sheehan and Clarke, the Algerians in Pontecorvo's film are "lackadaisical and passive" yet have an arcane "longer view of where they wanted to go." In other words, Algerians and Algeria contain a hidden historical revolutionary essence that winds itself through a three-thousand-year-old fervor. Such an essence is, as Said has pointed out, one of the principal tropes through which the Western world defines itself through and consequently against the Arab, or Eastern World (*Culture* 290–96).

This concealed, smoldering revolutionary essence is also suggested in a *New York* magazine article by Peter Rainer, who, although finding little historically comparable between the film and the war in Iraq, points out that Pontecorvo's Algerian protagonist, Ali La Pointe, leader of the FLN, "is not a character exactly, he's the embodiment of downtrodden Muslims clamoring for Liberation. Pontecorvo has a great eye for faces that carry within themselves a depth charge, and in Ali he gives us an unforgettable mask of suffering and rage. There is destiny in that acetylene glower of his, it tells us time is on his side." Rainer remarks that "not much in the current Iraq situation is historically comparable to the late-fifties Algerian struggle for independence dramatized in *The Battle of Algiers*, but its anatomy of terror remains unsurpassed — and, woefully, ever fresh." The dramatic images of an Arab epic of revolutionary stealth and terror steeped in *longue durée* — whether in comparison or through refusal of the comparison of Algeria and Iraq — constitute racialized codes. The images of a common terrorist character or type, whether within the context of anticolonial struggle or Iraqi insurgency, unite the understanding of the two geographical and political contexts and elide important historical distinctions. Ultimately, statements such as those found in Kaufman's report of the Pentagon's invitation to view "clandestine terrorists in places like Algeria and Iraq" suggest not only the concealed, ebullient nature of Arab terrorism but also the

Muslim nature of larger Arab insurgency. The anticolonial struggle for independence by the Algerian FLN becomes translated into the insurgency of Islamic fundamentalism. As Michael Chanan puts it in his brief review article of the film, "the trick is to see *The Battle of Algiers* as both a contemporary and historical film at the same time, which is not about the clash of civilizations" ("Outsiders" 40).[7] The comparisons made above, however, even when displaying attention to historical differences, ultimately elide the specificity of colonial history and, instead, substitute the meaning of its rebellion and victimization with Orientalist tropes.

Placed within the context of post–9/11, these tropes suggest a characterization of American hegemony as a neoimperialist practice. More importantly, much like the tactics of earlier colonial settlers, the Western practice of mapping out a space that seems alien yet visually enticing or appealing to the imperialist gaze can be seen in the Pentagon screening of the film. However, the specificity of this practice as a uniquely neoimperialist tactic is evidenced in the way commentary surrounding the film appropriated colonial history and, more specifically, victimization at the hands of anticolonial liberationists. The Pentagon's screening of *The Battle of Algiers* represents a unique moment in the history of the present, where, we might say, the apparatus of Western hegemony is laid bare. Certainly the Pentagon's screening displays the way that the representation of colonial history and of "third world" liberation might be positioned so as to inform a neoimperialist practice of mapping out territory to be occupied. It also reveals, however, the use of media from the colonial era in this process, and its exportation to the present for the purposes of identification, surveillance, and coding that prefigure, or at the very least, contemporaneously inform physical occupation of territory. The act of viewing the film as an analogous narrative of struggle demonstrates America's ability to abrogate the narrative of colonial history and its meanings for its own purposes and, moreover, exhibits its ability to use its paradigmatic images as a tactics of racialized codification of space and territory for its own narrative of hegemony.[8] While, as we will see below, the trope of victimization is central to Pontecorvo's treatment of the struggle for Algerian independence, the United States identified solely with its Arab enemy as victimizer, placing itself in the position of victim. The desire to occupy the victim's position so as to retaliate with victimization is central to the contemporary age of terror; it structures the "clash of civilizations" and is illustrated by the dynamics of spectatorship that the Pentagon viewing of Pontecorvo's film exemplified.

What is perhaps most interesting about the Pentagon screening of *The Battle of Algiers* is the way that colonial-era media was used in the wake of September 11 to reimagine the nation as a hegemonic power through the surveillance and control of victimization. If, as Benedict Anderson has argued, nations are imagined communities that establish themselves through a certain imagined image, then the process of reparation to the nation that took place in the wake of September 11 and in the Pentagon's viewing of *The Battle of Algiers* proved telling. Anderson defines a nation as "an imagined political community [that is] imagined as both inherently limited and sovereign" (6). What is key to Anderson's definition of sovereignty is his identification of its limited nature. Although Anderson does not address what occurs to a nation when the balance of its sovereignty and limitation is disrupted, as in the case of the United States in the wake of September 11 when the terrorist attacks created a sense of the limitations of its sovereignty, we might posit that a reimagination of sovereignty and its limitations would be in order. The screening of Pontecorvo's film and the discourses related to its release after September 11 suggest that the process of reimagining the nation in the wake of a disruption, or perceived disruption, of that nation's sovereignty is an integral component of the ongoing process of the imagined community. More importantly, perhaps, the screening in question suggested that the imagined control of victimization through visual mediation is central to the ways the imagined sovereign nation addresses the limitations of its sovereignty so as to reinforce it. By viewing and imagining victimization in Pontecorvo's film and in the terror of September 11 as a product of Arab terror only, not only did the United States ignore the limitations of Western sovereignty in its colonial history, it simultaneously appropriated the position of victim in the process of designating potential Arab victims. It is safe to say that this process reflects a larger Western process whereby the neoimperialism of the West establishes itself through the active reimagination of colonial history and the contemporary limits of Western sovereignty.[9] Central to these dynamics was the positioned control or imagined re-appropriation of Western surveillance and codification of its enemy. The Pentagon screening of Pontecorvo's film exemplifies how the continued re-appropriation of visual surveillance of the Other is an integral component not only of the appropriation of the victim's position and its ultimate transformation into that of victimizer but also of the process of reimagining the purview of geopolitical relations through the prism of the United States and the scope of its sovereignty.

We might say that Pontecorvo's film made explicit these spectatorial dynamics of the appropriation of terrorist victimization. After perhaps the film's most famous scenes where three consecutive bombs planted in the European quarter of Algiers by female terrorists have detonated, we witness the arrival of the French paratroopers led by the cool and impenetrable Colonel Mathieu, the image of whom bears an uncanny resemblance to Arnold Schwarzenegger's Terminator. Mathieu then holds a briefing of his troops, where the recent terrorist attacks are discussed. He begins by enumerating the escalating number of daily attacks faced by the French population of Algiers in recent days. He then issues a statement that not all of the Arab population is known or considered to be an enemy to the French presence, a speech that recalls official U.S. government discourses concerning Arab populations after September 11. After, he calls his men's attention to surveillance footage of the Arab populations, pointing out that continuous video is taken in select locations of the Casbah, the old labyrinthine neighborhood of Algiers populated largely by Arab citizens. As the soldiers watch, we view the projected black-and-white footage, akin to the film we are watching, and witness close-ups of passing veiled Muslim women and local men.[10] We then see searches in select entry points of the Casbah by French police. It is unclear in Mathieu's speech what the exact outcome of searches has been, but the implication of the scene is that visual surveillance of the Arab population might ultimately aid in the identification of the hidden enemy. More importantly, perhaps, this scene reveals how the surveillance and projection of Western measures of surveillance and policing are central to their own existence. This auto surveillance of Western practices of visual control reflects and reinforces, in a larger sense, the very spectatorial dynamics involved in the Pentagon screening of Pontecorvo's film.[11] Not only does this particular scene reflect clearly the types of racialized coding and surveillance of Arab populations put in place after September 11 by the U.S. government, it also mirrors the very dynamics of the Pentagon screening of the film itself. In a larger sense, viewed within the film being watched as surveillance footage, this scene suggests how the preexisting visual codes summoned to interpret the context of terrorism ultimately reflect those already in place beforehand.

The question remains as to what this type of process suggests for the condition of third cinema or resistance cinema today. As a classic film of nationalist struggle, *The Battle of Algiers* was widely received by critics as a "resistance" film. Whether characterized for its underscoring of the ambiguous nature of terrorism or for its direct message of anticolonial resistance, the film was widely applauded as an example of third cinema and as a resounding denouncement of terrorism. Jan Dawson, for instance, writes that "the most powerful — and ultimately the most persuasive — thing about *The Battle of Algiers* is its extraordinary fair-mindedness, its scrupulous refusal to simplify or romanticize the moral and practical choices on either side of the barricades" (52). Indeed, *The Battle of Algiers* does depict the brutalities of warfare on both sides. The film highlights the brutality of terrorist acts by the FLN just as it underscores the equally brutal French use of torture and repression. In one particular scene the

French plant a bomb in the Casbah near the home of an Algerian accused of murdering a police officer. The bomb explodes killing and injuring many innocent people. In reprisal Algerian women disguised as Europeans enter into the French quarter and detonate bombs in cafés and at the Air France terminal, killing and injuring many innocent victims in return.[12] During a press conference when captive FLN leader, Larbi Ben M'Hidi, is asked whether he feels that it is "cowardly to use women's baskets and handbags to carry explosive devices that kill so many innocent people," he responds: "And doesn't it seem to you even more cowardly to drop napalm bombs on defenseless villages, so that there are a thousand times more innocent victims? Of course if we had your airplanes it would be a lot easier for us. Give us your bombers, and you can have our baskets." In many ways this specular violence underscored by the film seems to align more closely with contemporary conditions of terrorism and reprisal despite the specific historical and contextual differences. Yet, ironically, the film's depiction of the ways that victim and victimizer ultimately both become terrorists is lost in recent analogies made between the Algerian and Iraqi contexts.

Roger Ebert writes of "the universal frame of reference" that the film establishes in its treatment of terror where "those not interested in Algeria may substitute another war." Writing in a similar vein of the pedagogical lessons the film provides, Pauline Kael states that "in none of the political melodramas that were to follow is there any sequence that comes near to the complex overtones of the sorrowful acceptance with which each of the three bomb-planting women looks to see who will be killed by her bomb." In all of these critical reviews the film's message as to the vicissitudes of terror as an imperialist tactic or as anticolonial struggle are highlighted. Yet, clearly, the film's complexities and indication of the gray areas of struggle between French forces and Algerian liberationists were lost during the Pentagon screening and, we might say, in the widespread commentary on the film that constructed a racialized perspective of pan-Arab terrorism.

Cinema of resistance, or third cinema, is conceived as a subversive aesthetic movement. Argentinean filmmakers Fernando Solanas and Octavio Gettino write that "what determines Third Cinema is the conception of the world, and not the genre or an explicit political approach. Any story, any subject can be taken up by Third Cinema. Third Cinema is a cinema of decolonization, which expresses the will to national liberation, anti-mythic, anti-racist, anti-bourgeois, and popular" ("Outsiders" 37). Distinguishing between first cinema in the commercial mode epitomized by Hollywood, and second cinema characterized by European *auteur* films, Solanas and Gettino posited that third cinema distinguished itself in opposition to these other two forms of cinema as a revolutionary aesthetic and highly charged political form.[13] Their conception of third cinema derived in great part from the experience of making the radical Argentinean documentary *La Hora de los Hornos* (The Hour of the Furnaces) in 1968. Since then, the leading theorist of third cinema, Teshome Gabriel, has proposed that the schema introduced by Solanas and Gettino tends to ignore certain imbrications of cinematic forms that lead to the creation of an interesting and challenging aesthetic. For Gabriel often the most interesting examples of third cinema are found in those films that occupy the gray zone in between. As such, third cinema is "moved by the requirements of its social action and contexted and marked by that strategy of action" ("Third Cinema" 40). Style becomes meaningful only in relation to the context of its use and in its ability to illuminate the ideology at work within a particular cultural context.

Third cinema, according to Gabriel, is thus not a demolition of Hollywood or *auteur* cinema but rather a dialectically inflected genre that provides "a rational interpretation of a historically defined reality so that a line of causation can be established" (*Third Cinema* 97). The conception of ideological positioning is important here since Gabriel characterizes third cinema as more than just a reality effect, or the projected impression of reality, but rather as the active and positioned interpretation of it. The praxis of third cinema, then, is one of confrontation with existing social realities: "The aesthetic of Third Cinema also moves between two poles; one, the demand that the works engage the actual pressing social realities of the day, and the other that the film achieve its impression of reality, not by simply mirroring, but by transforming the given" (*Third Cinema* 8). Key to Gabriel's formulation of the third cinema aesthetic is a certain engaged perspective. The third cinema filmmaker works from a postcolonial perspective, in the strictest sense, of liberation and politically representative engagement. The act of reimagining reality from the perspective of the filmmaker is germane to the production of third cinema; it hinges upon the interpretation of reality and constitutes a conscious surrender to the manipulative dynamics of the hermeneutic act.

Robert Stam and Louis Spence identify this quality of Pontecorvo's film best in pointing out its aberration from earlier portrayals of Algerians and its active partisan portrayal of the colonized liberation forces. Writing of the conventional suturing of the spectator to the colonialist perspective found in many films treating the destiny of the colonized, Stam and Spence point out that *The Battle of Algiers* exploited

> the identificatory mechanisms of cinema on behalf of the colonized rather than the colonizer. Algerians, traditionally represented in cinema as shadowy figures, picturesquely backward at best and hostile and menacing at worst, are here treated with respect, dignified by close-ups, shown as speaking subjects rather than as manipulable objects. While never characterizing the French, the film exposes the oppressive logic of colonialism and consistently fosters our complicity with the Algerians. It is through Algerian eyes, for instance, that we witness a condemned Algerian's walk to his execution. It is from within the casbah that we see and hear the French troops and helicopters. This time it is the colonized who are encircled and menaced and with whom we identify. (244)

Of course Stam and Spence interpret the film from a positioned perspective that shares the same political consciousness of decolonization they identify in Pontecorvo's film. Indeed, the crux of the question of engagement and realism derives from the cultural capital and political perspective that is a part of the apparatus of realism.

In his classic study *What is Cinema?* André Bazin points out this very problem, arguing that the very mise-en-scène of the classic neorealist style, for instance, reveals its own construction as a form politically engaged with its context. Writing of Vittorio De Sica's films, Bazin states, "Though this mise-en-scène aims at negating itself, at being transparent to the reality it reveals, it would be naïve to conclude that it does not exist . . . There is not one image that is not charged with meaning, that does not drive home into the mind the sharp end of an unforgettable moral truth, and not one that to this end is false to the ontological ambiguity of reality" (205). It is important to note that the comparison to the political slant found in the ambiguities of neorealism is not without basis since Pontecorvo's style was greatly informed by Italian neorealist aesthetics and principles by predecessors such as De Sica, Visconti, and Rossellini. His early filmmaking embraced the documentary style and the raw camera movement of neorealism in popular works such as *The Wide Blue Road* (1957) and *Pane e zolfo* (1959). Although neorealist intent might differ from the overtly liberationist character of *The Battle of Algiers*, which has become an emblem of third cinema, Bazin's formulation of the way the ambiguities of neorealist representation remain politically charged and open to appropriation by diverse ideologies is applicable to Pontecorvo's work. Writing of the political appropriation of De Sica's films in the post-fascist climate of Italy, Bazin points out the extreme polarity of interpretations found in ambiguous representations: "The ambiguities of *Miracolo a Milano* and *Ladri di Biciclette* have been used by the Christian Democrats and by the Communists" (207). In a similar manner we can say that the ambiguities underscored by Pontecorvo's film, the gray interstitial areas that unite torturer and tortured, victim and victimizer, ultimately folding them into a specular and singular equation, lend the film to appropriation by left- and right-wing ideologies alike.

Although Pontecorvo's ambiguous treatment of victimization contains the liberationist ideology associated with third cinema, it also lends its message, some forty years later, to appropriation by a Western power concerned with reimagining the limits of its hegemony and its status as victim of terrorist attacks. It is here that Bazin's notion of cultural capital in the apparatus of realism comes into play. For Bazin the spectator of the neorealist film brings to the screen's poetic and ambiguous representation of reality his or her own political imagination of it. We might go further to recall that the neorealist film also portrays, in the largest sense, victimization as a means of inciting spectatorial response. Perhaps the most emblematic scene of victimization in the neorealist film can be found in Rossellini's *Roma Città Aperta* (Rome, Open City). In the context of fascist Italy, immediately following the Nazi occupation, the scene of torture in Rossellini's film featuring the Marxist Manfredi, who is tortured by the Nazis to reveal information about the partisan movement in Rome, reflects the way that victimization in the neorealist film plays upon the cultural capital and political imagination of the nation as a victimized entity. Manfredi's torture by the Nazis, along with the Catholic Don Pietro's death as a martyr of the resistance, plays upon the preexisting cultural image of Italy as a nation victimized by the Nazis yet resistant in Marxist and Catholic values. In many ways the scene of torture in *Roma Città Aperta* capitalizes upon the prevailing sentiment of victimization to galvanize and codify Italian cultural values. Although victimization in Pontecorvo's film is portrayed differently, what the two examples share is the way that preexisting expressions of cultural values become affixed to the depiction of victimization when those values are perceived to be threatened.

The "Alger 1954" segment early in *The Battle of Algiers* is a salient example of a scene that lends itself to the identificatory mechanisms of preexisting Western conceptions of victimization in the wake of September 11. The neorealist documentary-style approach of Pontecorvo's camera focuses in on Ali La Pointe and his victimization at the hands of both French settlers and police. As the camera closes in on La Pointe's face while he is being dragged away by the police, the voiceover narration provides biographical details of his criminal history. While La Pointe's history is clearly embedded in the larger context of colonial oppression, the close-up shots of his face and the narrative of his criminality combine to play upon the idea of Western victimization at the hands of "Arab" terrorists. While this segment of the film, pointing as it does to the incipient nature of Algerian revolution in 1954, could clearly be read as an indictment of French colonialism that led to the police suppression and containment of Algerian independence, it can also be seen to align clearly with the perceived threat of victimization felt by the West in the aftermath of September 11. Moreover, the scene is preceded by the film's opening scene of torture where La Pointe's whereabouts are extracted. Even clear scenes of French victimization of Algerians in the film, such as the opening scene of torture and the subsequent roundup of Algerians in the search for La Pointe, can be read as necessary responses in a Manichean structure pitting perceived victim against victimizer. The still of La Pointe's face at the close of the opening segment of the film ends in a dissolve to the film's next segment about his criminality, symbolically pointing to the necessity of torture and "necessary means" as a response to Western victimization by a history of criminality. Moreover, the focus on La Pointe's face and the emphasis on his criminality mirror the practices of ethnic profiling that have become commonplace in the post–9/11 climate. Scenes such as these demonstrate how the cultural capital of the West, intent on appropriating the position of victim, could easily produce a viewing of the victim as victimizer and vice versa.

The ambiguities of Pontecorvo's treatment of terrorism amounted to more than just an occasion for the United States to codify Arabs according to age-old stereotypes and to interpret terrorism as an infliction affecting only the West. The Pentagon screening of *The Battle of Algiers* also offered the opportunity for the United States to work through the ambiguities of its own status as both torturer and victim. The ambiguities of Pontecorvo's film that signal the barbarism of both colonizer and colonized locked in a terrorist embrace proved the perfect imagery for the political praxis of the hegemonic nation faced with addressing the ambiguities of being at once victim and torturer. The working through of that ambiguous position corresponded perfectly to the exigencies of the moment, which called for an immediate valorization of not only sovereignty and the attending occupation of Iraq but also of all means required to achieve it. The screening of the film enabled a projection of the victim's position to occur and supersede the simultaneous position of torturer occupied by the United States at the time of the screening. Following Anderson's conception of the nation as an imagined community predicated on the ongoing imagination and activation of the limits of hegemony, we might say that the screening of Pontecorvo's film enacted the very process of reimagining the nation after September 11 as a victim. Of course the victim's position is the specular shadow of the torturer's position, the reverse side of the hegemonic equation. In this case the dominance of Western perspective and point of view are presumed and identified in *The Battle of Algiers* despite the ambiguities underscored by critics. That perspective, along with the cultural capital that informs it, is rooted in the ongoing imagination of the American nation that must transpose its positions as torturer and victim in order to galvanize its position as a hegemonic nation. The U.S. screening of Pontecorvo's film ultimately reveals how the resistance film can become the political screen onto which is projected the spectator's imagined image of hegemonic nationhood replete with a history of victimization and imagined reprisal.

Such conceptions of hegemony resonate with a larger history of European imperialist approaches to the Mediterranean. European colonialism in the Mediterranean attempted to impose the Western perspective as central in its occlusion of colonial history. And, as Chambers points out, the centrality of the control exercised by the

Western perspective within the history of colonialism in the Mediterranean resurfaces today in post–9/11 geopolitics: "This is why the destruction of the Twin Towers is the symbol of the epoch of global terror, rather than the eight thousand Muslims slaughtered by 'Christian' soldiers in Srebrenica or the hundreds of thousands exterminated in the genocide of Rwanda" (*Mediterranean* 20). One might add that the establishment of this worldview is based upon the idea of the victimization of the West by its Muslim "Other," rather than on a long history of Western imperialism. What becomes central, then, to the Western establishment of the centrality of 9/11 as the defining event of the age of terror is the establishment of Western victimization as a focal point.

The imagination of the hegemonic nation, as Anderson suggests, must constantly confront the limits and the strength of its sovereignty. The scenes of torture in *The Battle of Algiers* enabled just such a confrontation, particularly because of the way that torture in relation to American sovereignty had come to the forefront of political and public debate at the time with Guantanamo Bay. The opening scene of Pontecorvo's film takes place in a torture chamber where a captive member of the FLN is coerced to reveal the whereabouts of his leader, Ali La Pointe, after receiving repeated doses of electric shock. In a subsequent scene, following the arrival of French paratroopers in Algiers led by the Colonel Mathieu, torture becomes an official practice established without regard for French democratic measures. In a scene depicting a press conference, Colonel Mathieu remarks that "the word torture doesn't appear in our orders. We've always spoken of interrogation as the only valid method in a police operation directed against unknown enemies. As for the FLN, they request that their members, in the event of capture, should maintain silence for twenty-four hours, and then they may talk. So, the organization has already had the time it needs to render any information useless. What type of interrogation should we choose, the one the courts use for a murder case that drags on for months?" In many ways the U.S. government response to the torture of suspected members of al-Qaeda in 2002, before the screening of Pontecorvo's film, came to reflect the French response represented by Colonel Mathieu. The opening scene of the film corresponded to an image of the United States as torturer, a reality perceived as a necessary response to al-Qaeda threats after September 11, when U.S. sovereignty was interpreted as vulnerable and therefore limited.

Since 2002 the Guantanamo Bay detention camp has functioned as a military prison and interrogation camp for people suspected by the executive branch of the U.S. government of being al-Qaeda or Taliban operatives. Certain detainees no longer suspected are also held in the camp pending relocation. When reports of torture and abuse of detainees became public, open debate in the United States over torture began in earnest. Moreover, as an article by Paul Reynolds in the BBC titled "Papers Show U.S. Torture Debate" points out, debates over the definition and ethics of torture were taking place within the U.S. administration before such dilemmas became public. Detainees held by the camp were labeled "enemy combatants" by the Bush administration. This denomination placed the prisoners outside the limits of Article 3 common to the four Geneva Conventions that prohibited the use of torture and cruelty in the treatment of prisoners of war. Nevertheless, as Reynolds notes, the new thinking required by the contemporary war on terror needed to be consistent with the principles of Geneva. Bush's memo thus read that U.S. forces needed to treat detainees humanely. The war on terror was considered to be a war of intelligence that necessitated "interrogation." Yet, as Reynolds points out, military reports began to arrive from Guantanamo noting detainee resistance to U.S. interrogation techniques. As a result, the U.S. response to such reports changed and escalated, ranging from an altered definition of interrogation in August 2002 that encompassed severe physical pain to approved tactics of inciting fear in the detainee in November of that same year. In April U.S. defense secretary Donald Rumsfeld approved a memo that allowed for significantly increasing fear in the detainee, changing sleep patterns, isolation, and insult, amongst other tactics. Essentially, these internal government memos reveal an ongoing transformation and redefinition of the terms of interrogation to encompass conventionally defined torture. It is important to point out, though, that this process takes place over time as a function of received reports. The existence of such documents reveals the way that torture becomes an acceptable practice akin to interrogation when the limits of sovereignty are perceived to be exposed.

Of course we might say that the limits of sovereignty were perceived not so much as American territorial boundaries but rather as the boundaries of American Christian propriety eroded by Islam. Although the opening scene of torture in Pontecorvo's film might have reflected a certain image of America as torturer, a subsequent scene including the Algerian FLN communiqué as a voiceover in the film could be said to reflect the stakes of the war on terror for American sovereignty after September 11. That communiqué calls for "the restoration of the sovereign, democratic, and social Algerian state, within the framework of Islamic principles." Placed after the scene of torture, the communiqué functions to reinforce the justification for torture as a means of defending not only the democratic framework of America but also its fragile status as a Christian-based tradition.

While we might say that the Pentagon screening of *The Battle of Algiers* enabled the domestication of victimization, specifically its appropriation as something intrinsically inflicted on the West and, more importantly, America, we might also say that the implication of torture as a necessary tactic in the face of Muslim insurgents also bore witness to a domestication of the suggestion of the barbarism of torture that emerged in Guantanamo Bay. The screening of *The Battle of Algiers* enabled a recuperation of the terrorist tactics of the Arab enemy — viewed as vile and victimizing — and their subsequent translation into something intrinsically American and civilizing. Of course those same tactics would come into play in Abu Ghraib just months later, and it is easy to see how the Pentagon screening of *The Battle of Algiers*, placed as it was between two torture scandals, participated in the general climate that transformed or reimagined terrorism and torture as necessary tactics of the victimized.

In his memoir of torture during the Algerian War, Henri Alleg recounts the details of his victimization at the hands of the French. Alleg, a French journalist and member of the Communist Party that had allied itself with the FLN, was arrested by French paratroopers in 1957 and detained in an Algiers suburb. He was tortured systematically in order to reveal locations of important FLN leaders. In the preface of the book, Jean-Paul Sartre writes, "In looking at these two indissoluble partnerships, the coloniser and the colonised, the executioner and his victim, we can see that the second is only an aspect of the first. And without any doubt the executioners are not the colonisers, nor are the colonisers the executioners" (3). Although Sartre conceived of the relationship uniting colonizer and colonized, victimizer and victimized, as a function of racial hatred, his statements nonetheless reverberate with the contemporary "clash of civilizations." What structures the clash of civilizations in the age of terror is a fundamental drive to appropriate the victim's position, to identify fully and visibly with that position, and ultimately to transform it into that of the victimizer, so as to reestablish the nation's hegemonic position within the world.

The return of Pontecorvo's *The Battle of Algiers* to what, just years ago, might have seemed like a most unlikely audience, speaks volumes about the nature of post–9/11 politics and the condition of postcolonial resistance. The Pentagon screening of the film functioned as a cartographic process that mapped out the uncertain contours of the war in Iraq. The visible identification of al-Qaeda operatives proved difficult for the United States after the World Trade Center attacks. The faces of the victimizer were not readily available, and the profile was to be reconstructed, pieced together. The cinematic identifications that took place in the screening of

The Battle of Algiers and in reportage about it suggest that such identifications with Arabs as enemy combatants were facilitated by the liberationist narrative from forty years prior as well as by preexisting conceptions of Arabs that aligned more with racialized modes of perception.

Pontecorvo's film demonstrated that third cinema is as likely to be promoted by leftist ideology as it is to be appropriated as an example of right-wing persecution in the age of terror. What it revealed most, though, was the way that the trope of colonial victimization common to third cinema can be identified, controlled, and worked through for the purposes of victimization by a hegemonic power. Victimization was certainly at the heart of the colonial control of territory, but it did not always drive it. In the aftermath of September 11, victimization reveals itself to be a central tenant of the neo-imperialist drive for territory. It serves as a primary mode of identification and perception of the enemy, and it functions to justify that enemy's surveillance and control. Moreover, the screening of Pontecorvo's film proved to be an exercise in the way the limits of the hegemonic nation's own sovereignty and principles might be screened through colonial history and reimagined as victimized by cultural principles that appeared foreign and threatening. The end result of such a screening was a reinforcement of the imagined image of the nation that occluded the ambiguities of colonial history and ultimately used them to new imperialist ends.

Although Pontecorvo's film ends on a positive note of liberation, it did not imagine how the Algerians would ultimately come to replicate the very patterns of victimization and oppression that the colonial administration had instated. Indeed, the bureaucratic machinery of the colonial administration persisted long after formal independence with many Algerian state personnel owing their positions to the colonial administration. The FLN continued to allow France to maintain naval and air force bases in Algeria for a number of years after the Evian agreements in 1962. More importantly, perhaps, the Algerian state began a politics of extremism aimed at enforcing the rejection of Western cultural mores and values. The Pentagon screening of *The Battle of Algiers*, intended as it was to reimagine American hegemony in the wake of September 11, did not consider the limits of the historical scope of Pontecorvo's classic and, more importantly, the way the limits of the political imagination function in both art and reality.

What the return of *The Battle of Algiers* perhaps most saliently underscores is the way the political imagination mediated through the cinematic might fail in imagining its uses and historical trajectory. For instance it is unlikely that Pontecorvo ever imagined that his work would be appropriated some forty years later by a Western power for the purpose of better targeting Arab populations and ultimately facilitating what has amounted to a long-standing neoimperialist occupation. It is equally unlikely, however, that U.S. officials, in identifying with the surveillance, torture, and victimization depicted in Pontecorvo's film, would have imagined the limited reach of Western democracy that the existence of Pontecorvo's liberationist narrative ultimately underscores some forty years later. Those limits have now been made clear by the prolonged U.S. occupation of Iraq. While it would be easy to state that the return of *The Battle of Algiers* within the age of terror ultimately suggests the demise of third cinema, that conclusion too would fail to imagine the insistence of the limits of postcolonial narratives whose celebration of liberationist ideology has acquired a tainted and desultory tone.[14] The Pentagon screening of Pontecorvo's work demonstrates that given the new imperialist appropriation of postcolonial texts, it may very well prove to be more effective to see anticolonial works of resistance as indicative of the ways that the victimization highlighted in them engenders a struggle to assume the victim's position rather than to see them as works of imperialist resistance with direct currency today. In the current age of terror a problematization of victimization found in third cinema seems more effective than the postcolonial celebration of the representation of victimization as resistance. The return of *The Battle of Algiers* depicts with alacrity the limits of *realpolitik* aesthetics and the occlusion of colonial history and its legacy, but as an insistent indicator of the very limits of the postcolonial (and, indeed, neocolonial) imaginary to picture its own demise, it serves as a persistent and ever-important lesson for the history of the present.

2

Mapping National Identity and Unrealized Union

Rachid Bouchareb's *Indigènes*

In *Le Syndrome de Vichy* historian Henry Rousso identifies the return of memories that had been smothered under a reassuring myth of French national resistance during World War II as a period of time best captured by the image of "le miroir brisé" (broken mirror) (120). A number of developments after 1968, particularly during the period from 1972 until 1980, unsettled the mirror image of resistance that many French people had of the nation under occupation. Amongst the most significant developments, at least in terms of cinematic history, were the release of Claude Chabrol's *La Ligne de démarcation* in 1966, Marcel Ophüls's *Le Chagrin et la Pitié* in 1969, and Louis Malle's *Lacombe Lucien* in 1973. These works ushered in a new period when France's troubled relation to its wartime past became a central cultural concern manifested on screen. This period, according to Rousso, was then followed by an obsessive focus on the wartime experience, a national obsession exacerbated by high-profile trials, such as that of Klaus Barbie and the fiftieth anniversary of the "dark years" of the occupation (140–60). This retrospective gaze directed toward the experience of the occupation has been qualified as a nationalist vision steeped in tones of nostalgia and characterized as a fetishization of national memory. For Rousso and Eric Conan the prominence even of diverse and competing memories of the occupation signals "la sacralisation de la mémoire de la dernière guerre mondiale" (the sacralization of the memory of the last world war) and defines national memory by its "caractère paralysant" (paralyzing character) (44, 21). French nationalism emerges within this paradigm of memory as the obsessive search for national definition and character in vestiges of history. This search for national identity, as Richard Golsan points out, is observed not only in the terms of national introspection evinced by the retrospective national gaze but also in the fact that public debates related to the events of the occupation and its historical context have become defining features of political culture (23–29).

Upon first consideration it might seem inappropriate to insert Rachid Bouchareb's recent award-winning film *Indigènes*, written with Olivier Morelle, within the historical parameters set by Rousso. The film has been an immediate success since its release and competition in the category of Best Foreign Film at the 2007 Oscars. *Indigènes*, which translates to "natives" in French or, in this case, "indigenous soldiers" and has been attributed the English title *Days of Glory*, treats the overlooked role of North African soldiers in the French army during the liberation of France in the waning years of World War II and Vichy France. Tens of thousands of North African soldiers served for France, contributing to a larger total of roughly three hundred thousand colonized soldiers from Africa, Indochina, and other colonies; *Indigènes* is one of the first films to examine this topic in an epic and popular form, and it is certainly the first film treating this topic, as I will discuss below, to have been immediately influential within the political realm. In this chapter I examine the politicized nature of Bouchareb's portrayal of colonial-era victimization. Placing Bouchareb's work within the context of the 2005 riots in France, referred to as an exemplary instance of the "clash of civilizations," I examine how a return to the victimization of colonial history in the postcolonial revisionist account might occlude instances of contemporary neocolonial oppression related directly to the age of terror.

Indigènes invites instant comparisons with Bouchareb's award-winning film *Little Senegal* (2001). Bouchareb, who has referred to himself as a Franco-Algerian, was interested in the mapping out of histories of oppression related to the African experience of imperialism in his earlier film as well. *Little Senegal* follows the journey of a Senegalese guide, Alloune, who gives tours of the coastline where his ancestors were imprisoned and shipped to America in the Atlantic slave trade. One day Alloune travels to the plantations of the South in the United States in search of his ancestors, eventually locating descendants in New York City. While the focus in *Little Senegal* remains the search for ancestry within the imperialist space by the "native," the focus in *Indigènes* is the "native" and his relationship to imperialist space. However, much like *Little Senegal*, *Indigènes* too is an exercise in reliving and remapping the experience of imperialist displacement, if only in another direction.

The film follows, in a quite conventional Hollywood manner, the campaign of several North African soldiers who have enlisted in the army in 1943 as it travels northward from Morocco, Sicily, Provence, and the Vosges to its end in an Alsatian village. The treatment of this largely unrecorded history in *Indigènes* suggests a return to Rousso's conceptions of historical imagery, but one which takes into account the ways that the film, although treating one element of a largely subaltern and repressed history of World War II, also aspires to the image of French and North African identity united in the larger interest of the French nation. In this respect Bouchareb's project distinguishes itself from earlier treatments of the conscription of African soldiers during World War II, such as Ousmane Sembene's films *Emitai* (1971) and *Camp de Thiaroye* (1988), discussed below, which focus more specifically on the tragedy of colonial genocide in relation to Vichy France and the larger exploitative mechanics of the colonial calculus in the murder of colonized Senegalese villagers. Sembene's films, particularly *Camp de Thiaroye*, represent the growing consciousness of Senegalese soldiers of the turpitudes of the French national cause, relating the memory of Vichy anti-Semitism to larger patterns of colonial oppression. Focused as it is on promoting an understanding of the union of French and North Africans in the establishment of France's historical record of World War II liberation, Bouchareb's film is invested in putting North Africans on the French national map, both literally and figuratively.

In an interview with *Time*, Bouchareb, describing the group's retracing of the campaign route throughout France in its educational tour after the film, suggested that the film would foster an image of union in contemporary France by demonstrating how the North African soldiers were very much a part of the larger narrative of French national identity. Moreover, the film, according to Bouchareb, would instill a sense of pride and belonging in children of North African heritage living in France's troubled *banlieue*, one of the principal sites of widespread civil unrest in France during the latter part of 2005, as well as a larger sense of the parameters of French identity in other French citizens: "These kids from the *banlieue*, having reexamined this history, are going to get back the pride and dignity. And [the rest of the] French will see why these people are just as French as they are." This composition of the repressed and overlooked multicultural history of France's wartime experience in *Indigènes* suggests a reassembly of Rousso's broken mirror, an explicit attempt to bring together pieces of the repressed history of these colonized soldiers' service in such a way as to instill in the spectator a much larger sense of Frenchness.[1] Much like a reassembled broken mirror, a desired image for union and recognition emerges as an outcome of historical revisionism in *Indigènes*, but like a broken image, any seamless vision of such national unity ultimately remains impossible and unrealized within the film's diegesis. Yet, what is of most interest here is the way the film aspires to expand the boundaries of national identity through a retrospective gaze that underscores the impossible union between French and North African subjects within the film.

While one would not expect an unfractured image of national union to appear between the colonized soldiers and their French counterparts given the historical context of French colonialism, the film's focus on a unified and intransigent national unit of North African soldiers in the face of such fractured realities is significant in light of its final message.[2] The film's reassembly of the image of French national union into a coherent yet shattered mirror through its treatment of this occluded history, I will argue, plays an important role in our understanding of its politicized nature and its influential reception. Focus on the impossible union of North African soldiers and the French within the context of France's history of liberation in *Indigènes* is tied to a form of sentimentalism that plays on the demystification of French identity and France experienced by the North African soldiers. In this case the sentimental is engendered by the film's various representations of failed union between the soldiers and France and its citizens. The representation of the process of discovery of France by these men, and the accompanying realization of their intangible connection with its preconceived essence within the larger narrative of sacrifice for French liberty, function to create affective identification between the spectator and the soldiers that the film follows.

After a private viewing in the Elysée Palace on 5 September 2006 of *Indigènes*, which ends in an indictment of the low pensions received by France's "foreign" soldiers, Jacques Chirac and his wife, Bernadette, were reportedly moved by the depiction of colonized soldiers sacrificing all for little recompense. Indeed, the pensions of at least eighty thousand of France's colonized soldiers who fought in the French army were frozen in 1959, lagging far behind those of French soldiers. However, on September 27, one day before the official French première of *Indigènes*, Chirac announced that the French government would bring the pensions in line with those of French soldiers, committing an estimated four hundred million euros per year to the policy. One of the central issues that emerges from this alignment of politics and art is the general question of how the film's portrayal of this part of history was able to exercise such political appeal. Of course it is important to recall that Chirac's announcement came less than a year after the beginning of riots and civil unrest in October 2005 that involved French citizens of North African heritage. In fact Chirac's announcement on the twenty-seventh day of the month can be understood as a symbolic reference to the beginning of the riots in Clichy-sous-bois on October 27 one year prior. The film's release and subsequent viewing by Chirac so relatively soon after such civil discord are clearly important factors in the shaping of governmental policy.

The outbreak of the 2005 riots corresponded to an international mapping of French spaces of victimization defined, by and large, as those areas where the burning of cars and the destruction of property took place. Events spread to the metropolitan *cités* and HLM, or low-cost housing projects, in various parts of France after the accidental deaths of two teenagers, Zyed Benna and Bouna Traoré, in Clichy-sous-Bois in the eastern suburbs of Paris. Benna and Traoré were chased by the police and tried to hide in a power substation where they subsequently died of electric shock. Confined to urban areas for the most part, and affecting all fifteen of France's large *aires urbaines*, the rioting did affect some rural areas. Thousands of vehicles were burned, and close to three thousand rioters in total were arrested. In the various maps of the riots that emerged, the media represented destruction in icons of small fires or other symbols of danger or victimization. These symbols appear around the hexagonal map of France and underscore the spread of vandalism and violence. Most importantly, perhaps, the maps all supplement narratives about the *cités* as sensitive urban areas that have revolted to victimize the larger national space. In this way they participate in larger discourses and stereotypes about the victimizing impulses of ethnic minorities residing in these zones.[3]

What is most interesting for our discussion of Bouchareb's film and its particular engagement with national space, identity, and victimization is the complex relationship between the spaces of victimization represented by the riots and their mapping and the aura of colonial history that emerged at the time of the riots. Of course the riots of 2005 were not significantly new; they have plagued the areas commonly identified as the troubled *banlieues* in France's metropolitan concentrations for many years. These areas are frequently inhabited by France's marginalized population, immigrants from the Maghreb and other former French colonies and their children. Mathieu Kassovitz's film *La Haine*, *Hate*, is perhaps the most popular representation of the disenfranchisement of France's youth in the *banlieue*. It is also a film that depicts clearly ongoing instances of police abuse and the failures of the French system of *intégration*.[4] Moreover, it is a film that is vested in the contest over national space in its portrayal of urban tensions and police abuse in that, as Tom Conley argues, "its meaning moves from police to *polis* and from *polis* to cosmos" (190). Similar to the riots of 2005, *La Haine* maps the relationship between postcolonial urban encounters and national surveillance of space (read, ethnic surveillance by the police) in its attempt to establish the map of a new postcolonial cosmogony through the tropes of violence, rebellion, and metropolitan focus. This is not to say that the violence of the riots is to be equated with the representation of urban violence in *La Haine*. However, both film and event demonstrate the claims for space and voice that emerge within the tropes of victimization common to both.[5]

In one of the film's most violent scenes in the police headquarters, the camera centers on Sayid and Hubert handcuffed and chained to two chairs. Maps of urban quadrants in the background frame the torture of the two youths by the police that takes place in the foreground. The symbolic connection between the mapping of victimization within urban spaces and a national conception of ethnic space as a place of victimization is underscored in this way. The surveillance of ethnic spaces and their victimization then becomes intertwined with colonial history in a direct reference made by one of the police officers. Beating Hubert, one of the officers urges him to use his feet to pick up an object, the way it is done in his *pays* or country. The film's focus on neocolonial attitudes and policies of the police notwithstanding, this reference clearly points in a larger sense to the shadow of colonial history, slavery, and victimization that structures the tensions of French social and ethnic spaces. The metropolitan focus of the police headquarters in this scene recalls the opposition of a national metropolitan colonial administration to its "peripheral" colonial spaces. I evoke this scene from *La Haine* in relation to the 2005 riots and to Bouchareb's film because of its focus on the relationship between national space and its mapping out of boundaries and the clear references to colonial history and administration, a principal focus of *Indigènes*. While *Indigènes* raises the question of the relationship between colonial conceptions of national space and the place or space of ethnic minorities in France, such as the Maghrebi youth targeted by Bouchareb, so too did the riots invoke the question of an underlying colonial conception and administration of the French national space in 2005.

When, after nearly two weeks of ongoing riots had spread across much of France's marginalized urban periphery, French prime minister Dominique de Villepin issued a "state of emergency" across more than a quarter of national territory, he instated a measure derived from the 1955 colonial-era law designed to curb support for the Algerian war of national liberation. The measure afforded prefects the unquestionable right to establish curfews and granted the interior minister the possibility of undertaking search-and-seizures, censorship of the press, and the closure of public spaces. Applied in Algeria proper for a period of six months during France's colonial occupation, the law had been put into effect on only three other occasions prior to the 2005 riots: twice in France during the Algerian War and once in 1984–85 in French New Caledonia to suppress an indigenous liberation movement. Roughly a week after the declaration of the state of emergency on November 15, the National Assembly, with strong support from Villepin, Sarkozy, and President Jacques Chirac, voted to extend the measure for an additional three months. This deployment of the colonial law points to a clear return to colonial administration transposed within the boundaries of postcolonial metropolitan France.

Contemporary French urban centers function in opposition to their impoverished peripheries where the riots began, areas further marginalized by their description in state policy, the media, and popular imagery as being racially and culturally different from mainstream France.[6] This structural opposition recalls that of colonial settler areas in relation to "indigenous" zones of colonial space. Deployment of the colonial law thus created further resonances with colonial administrative policies in the sovereign policing of peripheral areas.[7] For the most part, initial observations of the confrontations read the events as manifestations of a larger "clash of civilizations," linking them to the Palestinian *intifada* and the Iraqi insurgency while seeking the role of terrorist organization within them.[8] However, as Paul Silverstein and Chantal Tetreault argue, "social life in the housing projects in question is marked precisely by a lack of effective organizational bodies or unifying ethnic or religious ideologies." As opposed to explanations of anti-imperialist Arabism or anti-Western activism offered by some commentators, more plausible explanations were evident in social issues such as rampant unemployment, police harassment, racial discrimination, and the failure of social infrastructures, such as the school systems.[9] The failure of France's policy of integration of migrant populations from Africa, the Caribbean, and Southeast Asia is clearly at the heart of this matter.

As the integration policy failed, forceful targeting and surveillance, the mapping of ethnic victimization, one might say, became standard practice. In 2003, responding to previous riots in "sensitive" areas with concentrations of ethnic minorities in France, Sarkozy ordered an increase in Socialist Prime Minister Lionel Jospin's deployment of seventeen thousand military gendarmes and thirteen thousand riot police to patrol these "sensitive urban zones." The increase in troops constituted part of Sarkozy's post–9/11 war on terror. However, the clear targeting of Arab and "Beur" youths in the *cités* and HLM was also a result of this measure. A recent image on the newly released version of *La Haine* in DVD format featuring Sarkozy's face plays on the implication of France's current administration in the targeting of marginalized populations in the *cités*. The cover of the DVD revises the eerie refrain from *La Haine*, "jusqu'ici tout va bien" (up till now everything is going fine), to read "jusqu'ici tout allait bien" (up till now everything was going fine), and implicates Sarkozy, Villepin, and Chirac in the construction of a scenario of complacency with regard to civil problems in the *banlieue*. The title, *Hate*, taken with the theme of the film, places the blame on the current French administration for a continuous cycle of violence and civil unrest that ultimately led to the 2005 riots and equates the administration with France's prominent right-wing voice Jean-Marie Le Pen.

Further targeting of Arab and Muslim populations preceding the riots was witnessed in the March 2005 ban on Muslim headscarves and other ostensible religious symbols in public schools. The ban was crafted in the name of promoting citizens' equal access to secularism, but the result seemed to be a targeting of the Muslim population since roughly two million children in France are educated in Catholic schools that receive 80 percent of their budget from the government. These symbolic practices work with currents of economic marginalization to further spatially marginalize the *cités*. The spread of the riots to other urban areas in France can be understood as a result of the triple force of marginalization: symbolic, economic, and spatial. The riots, therefore, can be seen as an attempt to reclaim national space from the economic, symbolic, and administrative control that has led to the repeated victimization of France's marginalized ethnic communities.

It is interesting, then, that President Chirac's reaction to his viewing of *Indigènes* roughly a year after these riots encompassed a material political gesture toward France's formerly colonized soldiers. Given the context of the failure of France's social structure with respect to, in particular, its populations of North African heritage and origin, we have good reason to view Chirac's gesture with a measured and healthy degree of skepticism, particularly in the aftermath of the 2005 riots. Moreover, we might also ask what this national gesture might really do to resolve many of the social tensions manifested by the riots. At the same time, even as we laud *Indigènes* for its wider appeal and success, we must also ask questions about the film that led to its successful reception. Influence on governmental policy notwithstanding, the film's success raises the question of the degree to which a particular aestheticization and thematization of history necessary to such ends might ultimately diverge from the convergent national complexities and traumas of Vichy France and French colonialism. While that may very well be the topic of yet another film, it is pertinent to ask how the film's thematics and sentimentalism function so persuasively and what particular vision of collective memory the film ultimately promotes. How, in mapping the role of North Africans and their ultimate victimization by governmental policy in the way it does, might we understand the film's contribution to revisionist history? Does the film's cartography of victimization point to an attempt to solicit a profound awareness of the relationship between the national political landscape that has permeated colonial metropolitan France and the realities affecting younger generations of Maghrebians, immigrants, and new ethnicities affected by the current political landscape?

To begin to treat these questions, we must consider how the North Africans' desired yet impossible union with the French promotes identification with their position as active participants in a French national narrative from which they are also excluded. Loyalty to France in the face of the fractures of cultural identity and politics, particularly under colonial rule, remains an overriding theme of the film. The film's representation of the ambiguities and frequently arbitrary nature of a colonial system that at once enlisted men as cogs in a national war machine and excluded them from the same treatment as the French is unequivocal. North African soldiers receive food of poorer quality; they do not benefit from the same winter clothing; they are frequently berated as insubordinates; the French press credits French and not North African soldiers for securing heroically the Alsatian outpost, and so forth. In his review of the film for the Cannes film festival, Kirk Honeycutt remarks, "If there is one thing you wish Bouchareb might have included is a scene or even a line in which one of his North African characters would explain this loyalty to a country that does not always return that loyalty." Perhaps one of the most obvious scenes depicting such loyalty is evidenced in the soldiers' resounding chorus of the Marseillaise in front of the French flag, a scene the irony of which recalls a homologous moment in Jean Renoir's *La Grande Illusion*. While Honeycutt is correct to point out that there is no explicit commentary on loyalty made during the film, there are moments of questioning and dissent, but often these moments are little more than muddled confusion on the part of the soldiers rather than a full-blown existential crisis. The absence of any explicit explanation plays into the film's representation of the active nature of the soldiers' sacrifices, action based on loyalty to the French cause. In many ways Bouchareb's film can be understood as a mapping of the victimization of these loyal North African soldiers by a country that has no room in its national narrative for them. This image of loyalty is reinforced and rendered more salient when one considers the various disillusionments of the North African soldiers who expect to connect fully with France and its people. The nature of such individual connections encompasses diverse social relations, including male kinship and cultural sharing, romantic love, career advancement within the French system, and public recognition, amongst others. The cartography of this disillusionment in metropolitan France spreads from the documented movements of the soldiers from the south to the north of the entire country, further underscoring how the entire national space is implicated.

The first of such instances of disillusionment in *Indigènes* can be seen in the relationship between Messaoud (Roschdy Zem) and

Irène (Aurélie Eltvedt), a young woman from Marseille. Messaoud meets Irène when the campaign arrives at Marseille; she is charmed, we are to believe, as much by his physical prowess as by his exploits in previous battles. Although the lovers become separated when the campaign must forge on to the north, Messaoud carries in his helmet a picture of his lover and sends letters to her. Irène reciprocates by sending love letters to Messaoud. However, the letters never reach the lovers as French administration intervenes to censure them. Irène goes so far as to inquire with French authorities about Messaoud, only to have us discover that the administration is hostile to relations between North Africans and French women. The impossibility of the couple's multicultural union is finalized when Messaoud is killed in the Alsatian village along with all other members of the group we follow, with the exception of one soldier, Abdelkader (Sami Bouajila). The irony of this failed union is further accentuated by the fact that the North African soldiers die fighting for the sake of Alsatians, whose status, both culturally and legally, is also exceptional in relationship to both France and Germany.

The second important instance of unrealized multicultural union underscored by the film is witnessed in the relationship between Said (Jamel Debbouze) and Sergeant Martinez (Bernard Blancan), who is quick to defend his men when confronting his superior officers but reluctant to ever utter an encouraging word to his own unit. Said, who is motivated to return home to his mother, becomes an assistant to Martinez, discovering that the sergeant keeps a picture of his own mother, a North African woman, in his pocket. When asked to share a drink of whiskey with Martinez, Said decides to broach the topic of the kinship the two men share. Not only are they united by a devotion to the maternal figure but they are also united as Algerians, according to Said. As a "French" soldier, Martinez is enraged as much by the suggestion of parity as he is by the disclosure of his North African roots. He violently orders Said to never speak of the matter again and expels him from his quarters. Ultimately, the picture Martinez keeps near his heart in his shirt pocket appears as taboo as the picture of Irène carried in Messaud's helmet. In this way images of multicultural connection, mediated by both reason and emotion are ultimately impossible.

Unfinished here, the history of unrealized union between Said and Martinez becomes even more complex as the film progresses. When the campaign arrives in the Alsatian village with Martinez, who was gravely wounded in the Vosges, Said tells him in an angered tone of his wish that Martinez will die. However, when the group comes under heavy German attack during the final battle scene in Alsace, Said makes a desperate attempt to enter the farmhouse and extract Martinez from his bed. Both soldiers are then killed by enemy fire. As the camera tracks Corporal Abdelkader, the lone survivor of the campaign, we discover with him the bodies of the two soldiers next to each other on the ground. This unofficial memorial scene without entombment demonstrates the unrealized union of the French and North African soldiers and encapsulates, in a larger sense, the symbolic unrealized union and memorial of this overlooked history within the official vision of France's World War II experience. The irony of the deaths of Said and Martinez on common ground is further underscored by the fact that Martinez, a pied-noir of European origin (Spain, as suggested by his name) and Said, an Arab, both born in Algeria, represent two very different trajectories in relationship to colonial history in Algeria. Given that European colonists who obtained French citizenship received legal rights that Arabs did not, the deaths of Said and Martinez function further as an ironic marker of unrealized union.

The film's final scene at a military graveyard in Alsace, shot from the perspective of the contemporary period, attempts to establish a symbolic union within the framework of collective national memory as a now aged Abdelkader visits the tombs of both Said and Martinez. Like the memorial scene at the close of Steven Spielberg's *Schindler's List*, this scene too positions the spectator in such a way as to understand a desired yet impossible union, an intimate relation tainted by an unbridgeable distance, in this case between these North African soldiers and the larger notion of French national identity. This memorial scene attempts a recuperation of the death scene of the Alsatian village and enacts a ritualistic and symbolic union on French soil of the unrealized union of North African soldiers and the French during World War II, and from that period until the present.

As a site of national memory, the military graveyard represents what Pierre Nora identifies as a quintessential site of memory, a national *lieu de mémoire*. However, as Nora is quick to point out, one of the characteristics of the *lieu de mémoire* as a national marker of collective memory is its ability to signify new referents of ethnic and national identity: "le lieu de mémoire est un lieu double; un lieu d'excès clos sur lui-même, fermé sur son identité et ramassé sur son nom, mais constamment ouvert sur l'étendue de ses significations" (the memory site is a double site; a site of excess closed upon itself, locked into its identity and bolstered by its name, but constantly open to the spectrum of its significations) (42). Understood this way the cemetery as a site of national memory becomes a space where the type of unrealized union highlighted in the film might be recuperated as a belated multicultural ideal. National history as a memorial site might thus broaden to establish, as it were, a more perfect union. As Nora points out, *lieux de mémoire* are first and foremost haunting remainders of history, "des restes . . . intimement noués de vie et de mort, de temps et d'éternité" (remains . . . intimately tied up in life and death, in time and eternity) (28). As such, the cemetery scene, while providing symbolic union on French soil, also haunts with the aura of the impossible union created by the realities of colonial injustice. The deaths of these soldiers, although marked by loyalty to the French cause of liberation, are also marked by French colonialism. Incorporation into the French national memory site of liberation can only take place through this haunting remainder of World War II history as well. The scene thus symbolically states that these soldiers are very much a part of the history of French national identity and yet, as such, are forever subject to an unrealized union. Framed with a subsequent shot of Abdelkader's return to miserable living conditions, this scene serves as a prelude to an extra-diegetic commentary on the history of the soldiers' pensions. The effect of this symbolic recuperation of unrealized union is to appeal to the sense of national unity and simultaneous injustice that the film underscores throughout.

A third poignant instance of unrealized union related to the disillusionment of North African soldiers is embodied in the figure of Corporal Abdelkader. Abdelkader believes fully in the mission of France and, particularly, in its civilizing values. He is quick to call his unit to order reminding them of the benefits of civility and the principles of the French Revolution. He is optimistic that the only path to redemption is through an embrace of Frenchness as a liberatory and civilizing ideal. However, as the film progresses we see that, regardless of Abdelkader's great success, no promotion is possible within the ranks of the French army. Martinez himself remarks that Abdelkader merits promotion as much as anyone. Although Abdelkader ultimately survives the ordeal of the liberation campaign, the film's final suggestion of his years of misery in living conditions incommensurate with his service reveals a greater disillusionment. Moreover, the film's message about the frozen pensions of these soldiers demonstrates that not even the slightest official recognition for his service was ever made by the French system in which he believed so firmly.

A salient example of this lack of recognition is obvious earlier in the film at the end of the Alsatian battle as well. As Abdelkader begins to leave the village where all members of his squadron have been massacred in a shorthanded battle against a larger German contingent, French reinforcements finally arrive. The aporia between official and local recognition is apparent when French soldiers pose for official press photos and answer questions about the campaign, receiving glory for a battle they never even witnessed. As Abdelkader slowly leaves the village, a smattering of applause and congratulations is offered by the Alsatian villagers, whose lives his unit saved. Here, unrealized union between an official French system of public recognition and the North African soldiers is underscored. This specific example of unrealized union reveals, in a much larger sense, how the archival system responsible for inscribing this history into official public record, and therefore for establishing public recognition, ultimately failed to include all of those involved in the French national cause and its narrative. The occluded history of these soldiers, excluded from any official public recognition, is thus brought to the foreground as the failures of the French system of historical inscription are indicted.

The above instances of disillusionment and unrecorded history are framed symbolically to make the audience understand the soldiers' passage from belief in union with France to eventual disillusionment. Aerial shots of the regions of the campaign, beginning with Morocco and moving northward, announce each shift in movement of the unit. These shots fade slowly from black and white to color as clouds move past. This fairly commonplace cinematic device performs a specific role as it suggests the shifts in the soldiers' beliefs and expectations in a France they had never seen (in black and white) to the colored realities of failed union that the entire country ultimately offers as the campaign traverses France. The aerial position places the spectator in the privileged position of omniscient viewer and in this way establishes him or her as having complete insight into the unrealized unions that were so much a part of these soldiers' expectations of France. The shifts in color also function to signal symbolically that what we are viewing is real history, not simply a faded and incomplete archive like that composed of the black-and-white photos the press took of only the French soldiers. Coupled with the aerial perspective, these shifts to color ultimately suggest that we will be viewing a more complete version of history, the real inclusive version.

This reality effect is witnessed in the wide lens battle scenes as well. Indeed, the resonance with Hollywood is particularly evident in Bouchareb's comments: "Until now France has made films about the Resistance, but no World War II films like the Americans have made, like Spielberg's *Saving Private Ryan*." Referring to successive generations of North African immigrants, Bouchareb remarks, "Our movie, too, now shows that the grandparents of these young people liberated France . . . along with Tom Hanks." Clearly, the reference point for sentimentalism and cinematic identification concerning this history remains rooted in a Hollywood tradition, a move that interestingly attempts to bridge culturally specific and overlooked histories with a spectatorship accustomed to Hollywood cinematic style and subject.

Although the majority of the film makes the appeal to Hollywood-formed sensibilities through wide lens scenes and color, the opening credits diverge from this tendency while simultaneously functioning to communicate that what we are about to see is part of a much larger vision of French culture. As the opening credits roll, images Bouchareb obtained from archived images taken from Algerian television appear. Framed as stills, the images recall the black-and-white "scènes et types" of North African life featured on colonial postcards that were commonly sent to France during the period of French colonial rule.[10] The images feature different scenes of everyday "indigenous" life and activity. The reference to indigenous here is made expressly because the images featured from Algerian television are clearly positioned so as to reference the history of the colonial gaze, its postcard appropriation of everyday North African life as an authentic, exotic, and indigenous difference in contrast to French culture. The position of these scenes as the very first images the viewer encounters establishes the tone of the film's larger message of fractured union and partial historical vision. These indigenous scenes, so common to colonial history, represent only one very limited way of seeing North Africans in contrast to what the film's consecutive scenes of *Indigènes* will offer. With these opening images the filmic narrative positions the spectator's gaze behind the historical colonial lens where North Africans are viewed as passive objects of colonial history rather than as active agents of a national defense. The film's portrayal of the campaign then reverses this equation, placing the North Africans in a position of active, albeit excluded, agency within the French nation. Here, as elsewhere, the film transmits the message of how these soldiers are excluded from the national narrative by the official record of French history yet actively involved in its very composition.

Indigènes is one of few films to exercise an immediate influence within the political realm, and for this it distinguishes itself. The film's focus on unrealized union between North African soldiers and France and its spectatorial positioning aspire to an inclusion of the soldiers who served France as well as to the inclusion, according to Bouchareb, of a much larger population of North African origin and heritage within the larger reflection of French national identity. Appeal to the spectator through a sentimentalism based upon the idea and cause of the nation, and the limits of its inclusion, has been influential not only on the political front but also within the artistic realm. The film's ensemble of actors, including Bernard Blancan as Martinez, received the best actor award at Cannes, suggesting once again the important image of union.

Given this appeal, it is worth considering what vision of collective memory is promoted by the film and how the cartography of victimization it presents might be understood in relation to colonial history and its aftermath. Recent years have witnessed a surge in attempts to reconsider the role of colonialism within the history of former European imperialist nations. France has been no exception. According to Patrick Weil, "La perception de l'histoire des autres, leur intégration dans l'histoire nationale, c'est l'exigence ultime et nécessaire de la diversité dans la République" (The perception of the history of others, their integration into national history, is an ultimate and necessary exigency of diversity in the Republic) (Introduction). Echoing Weil, the introduction to a recent collection of essays, *La Fracture coloniale: La société française face au prisme de l'héritage colonial*, aspires to a reconsideration of the image of French national identity.[11] The idea for the collection is underpinned by the concept of broadening the parameters of the nation and what it means to belong to it from the perspective of the role played by colonial history: "il est utile d'évaluer les consequences actuelles des héritages de la période coloniale, pour des millions de femmes et d'hommes issus de cette histoire, mais aussi pour l'ensemble des Français" (it is useful to evaluate the current consequences of the legacies of the colonial era, for millions of men and women whose history this is, but also for the entire French nation) (27). For the authors of this text, as for Bouchareb, the colonial fracture, the impossible union of France with its colonial heritage, has impeded a more inclusive vision of the French nation to emerge in all its realities.

While this is certainly a legitimate concern of historical revisionism, it is possible that the memorial process itself, focused as it is in Bouchareb's film on national cause and composition, may actually overlook the real historical trauma that brings the filmic narrative into existence in the first place. Writing of the "emplotment" of historical events related to national identity, Eric Santner identifies a tendency of a certain narrative focus in film and literature to either overlook completely or, at the very least, underplay the reason for the existence of national trauma in the first place. While the specific focus varies, it almost always underplays one or more of the crucial reasons for the very existence of the narrative: "By narrative fetishism I mean the construction and deployment of a narrative consciously or unconsciously designed to expunge the traces of the trauma or loss that called that narrative into being in the first place . . . Narrative fetishism . . . is a strategy of undoing, in fantasy, the need for mourning by simulating a condition of intactness, typically by situating the site and origin of loss elsewhere" (144). Though Santner is discussing representation of the trauma of the Holocaust in relation to national identity, his identification of the ways that the underpinnings of a national trauma might be overlooked by a certain type of narrative is relevant for our understanding of collective memory in Bouchareb's film. Narrative fetishism becomes a concern when we consider that the focus of *Indigènes* remains the cause of the French nation and the necessity of symbolically incorporating the North African soldiers into the French narrative of national identity. Understood this way we begin to see how the trauma of colonialism and the loss of life it entails as an integral part of French history underpinning this film are underplayed in favor of a gesture toward union to which the filmic narrative aspires.

As a *lieu de mémoire* of national identity, *Indigènes* does open the concept of the French nation to a wider understanding. As a memory site of national identity, it also remains more focused on the composition of the nation, on the reassembly of the "broken mirror" of national identity, rather than on the instrumentality of the nation that leads to the loss ultimately engendered by exclusionary practices.[12] This occurs primarily through the film's emphasis on the campaign for the national cause of liberation and the message that all those who sacrificed for it must be considered a composite of the nation's identity. In their critique of "positive images" of the colonized, Robert Stam and Louis Spence point out that even postcolonial representations that focus on positive, rather than distorted, cinematic images of the colonized can prove problematic: "We should be equally suspicious of a naïve integrationism which simply inserts new heroes and heroines, this time drawn from the ranks of the oppressed, into the old functional roles that were themselves oppressive, much as colonialism invited a few assimilated 'natives' to join the club of the elite" (241). The soldiers in *Indigènes*, devoted as they are to the French national cause, serve as heroes for a national narrative that, in the context of the post 2005 riots in France, requires a focused scrutiny that is impossible given the emphasis on heroism and integrationism in Bouchareb's film. While *Indigènes* does not constitute a naïve integrationism, in that its intent is clearly to raise consciousness of colonial history, its focus nonetheless remains the insertion of new heroes into the French national narrative, when it is that very narrative itself which requires criticism.

In 1971 and 1988 Sembene's films *Emitai* and *Camp de Thiaroye* were released, films which turn to the relationship between French national identity, colonial and Vichy France, and the conscription of African soldiers. Both films, serving as chapters in the tragic story concerning the Casamance region, the region of Sembene's birth, focus on the growing awareness of colonized Senegalese soldiers of the very limits of the paradigms of French national identity and instrumentality. Moreover, these films represent a coming to consciousness on the part of the soldiers of the necessity of making a clear distinction between service to the French national ideal and the oppression of colonial subjugation, which was also a part of that ideal. In *Emitai* France's civilizing mission, the *mission civilisatrice*, is revealed to be an instrument of genocide. Although the focus of Sembene's films here differs from that of *Indigènes* in their emphasis on one bloody event in Senegal, I believe it is important to turn to those films as predecessors in the treatment of colonial victimization in a discussion of the World War II era. A brief consideration of *Emitai* and *Camp de Thiaroye* as precursors to the type of colonial revisionist history seen in *Indigènes* reveals the pitfalls of a cartography of victimization whose focus remains the composition rather than the instrumentality of national identity. In other words the comparative cartographies of victimization in these films enable a deeper understanding of how national space might be seen as a place where relatable and comparative political dimensionality might be better underscored. In the context of the release of *Indigènes*, this is particularly important given the backdrop of the 2005 riots and Chirac's political pronouncement on the pensions of colonized soldiers.

Emitai relates events that took place in the village of Effok in 1942 when a detachment of French troops of the Vichy regime shot dozens of unarmed villagers, including women and children, when they refused to hand over their rice crops to support the war effort. While the film critiques the brutality of the French army, into which young Senegalese men were forcibly drafted one year prior to the village slaughter, it also critiques the villagers' inability to defend themselves through their reliance on naïve mechanisms. In typical Sembene fashion, no tradition is spared critique. The village elders invoke ritual and spirits to defend themselves against military repression as the village women are tortured at the hands of the French to reveal the whereabouts of the rice crop. The historical context of this scene from 1942 is the transfer of allegiance to de Gaulle from Marshal Pétain by the colonial governors of French-held West Africa. Yet within the film, as John Downing has argued, "Sembene is pointing out with ineluctable logic that colonial policy and Fascist policy are indistinguishable if you are so unfortunate as to find yourself on the receiving end" (195). *Emitai* mapped, in a multidirectional manner, the calculus of Vichy Fascism and colonial oppression.[13] In the film's mapping of the brutality of the French national *mission civilisatrice* onto the analogous instrumentality of the Vichy regime, the film posed a clear threat to French soil. As Downing points out, the French government delayed the screening of *Emitai* on French soil for six years after its release and persuaded a number of other neocolonial regimes, particularly in West Africa, to ban the film altogether. The film's clear-cut portrayal of the victimization suffered by the colonized at the hands of the French during World War II represented a clear and present danger to the image of the French nation. *Emitai* thus represents a salient case of how the mapping of imperialist victimization, when completely unambiguous, may not only be open to interpretation by an imperialist power, as was the case with the Pentagon's screening and appropriation of Pontecorvo's *The Battle of Algiers*, but may also be easily wiped off the map completely. Yet, the comparison here to *Indigènes* is unmistakable, in that Sembene's film maps the space of colonial victimization during World War II as a complex component of the historical composition of national identity. Such a composition is historically directed toward specifically different yet comparative frameworks of practice: Vichy and imperialist France. While the focus in *Indigènes* remains the composition of French national identity and the broadening of national space to encompass that which had already proven itself to align with the best ideals of that space, *Emitai* focuses more on the critique of that which authorizes such boundaries or mappings of national identity.

Bouchareb's film does not incorporate a comparative critique of the instrumentality of French national practices of exclusion and, without a doubt, this has contributed to its positive reception in France. Yet, for the film to assure its director's goals of enabling a space for marginalized Maghrebi youths, it would seem that some gesture toward mapping the relationship of colonial-era practices of exclusion and impossible union to contemporary social conditions would be necessary, particularly since, as we saw in the outset of this chapter, colonial law is still summoned as a solution to civil problems in metropolitan France. While it is not my intent to dwell entirely on what Bouchareb's film did not do, it is relevant to ask what comparative cartographies of victimization in the films of Sembene and Bouchareb might illuminate.

Clearly, on a purely pragmatic level, a film like *Emitai* may be critiqued for the way its focus led the film to a near immediate exclusion from the French political realm. However, viewed now in resonance with Bouchareb's film, it is interesting to note how these different yet related maps of imperialist victimization complement one another in interesting ways. What the inevitable comparison produces is a commentary on the continued importance of diverse yet related mappings of the colonial experience. Taken together, the mappings of victimization offered by *Emitai* and *Indigènes* demonstrate how the historical underpinnings of victimization in different places and periods provide a comparative geography of imperialism in the postcolonial period, one that enables us literally to see the different claims that the representation of victimization makes about the victimizer and the victim. These maps, limited as they might be in their individual approaches, when compared, might enable a historical perception of the limits and possibilities of postcolonial critiques of the imperialist legacy. In other words the visual quality of these types of representation of victimization enables us to map together spaces of victimization in such a way as to see how the demands made about territory and victimization within it might fall short or ultimately succeed within a larger historical and spatialized postcolonial perspective. The visual quality of victimization within representations of space is important here since it ultimately underscores the material dimensions of space and subjects that are victimized. Although both films approach the topic differently, in *Indigènes* and *Emitai* we see the soldiers' exclusion from national space and the ultimate disillusions of their relationship to it. The material dimensions of victimization in relation to the imperialist project in both the metropolitan center and its colonial periphery can be mapped, plotted, and reviewed. Likewise, the comparison of the subjectivity of colonial victims in *Indigènes* and *Camp de Thiaroye* enables us to see different responses to imperialist victimization.

If *Emitai* reveals the French *mission civilisatrice* as a collective national effort analogous in many ways to Nazi horrors, *Camp de Thiaroye* underscores the subjectivity of the African *tirailleurs* in ways that lend interesting comparison to the subjectivity of the North African soldiers in *Indigènes*. In *Emitai*, as in *Indigènes*, the collective experience is foregrounded, and the conscripted soldiers are represented more as the mentally colonized accomplices of France. However, in *Camp de Thiaroye* the camera moves in and lingers on the faces of the individual soldiers we come to know, and their dilemmas are developed in ways that portray the complexity of being caught between loyalty to one's country and service to the French campaign.

Camp de Thiaroye picks up two years after the massacre in Effok, even though the film appeared seventeen years after *Emitai*. It focuses primarily on an episode that took place not far from Dakar in 1944 when African soldiers kidnapped a French general as a way of obtaining the pay that had been promised them. Upon the release of the general, the French military reprisal took the lives of many of these soldiers. The film focuses on the consciousness of Sergeant Diatta, a native of Effok whose parents had been killed in the massacre two years prior. On many levels the comparison between Diatta and Corporal Abdelkader from *Indigènes* is clear. Diatta, like Abdelkader, is a professional soldier with successful experience in Europe. He is well read and plans on continuing his education in France. He is a model of assimilation and evolution, like Abdelkader, and serves as a symbol of the relative success of "civilizing" values. He frequently expresses the strength of his soldiers to the French Captain Raymond, just as Abdelkader does with Sergeant Martinez. Yet, here, comparisons in the development of consciousness and subjectivity in the two soldiers begin to draw short.

Diatta, unlike Abdelkader, is aligned more solidly, if not hesitantly, with uprising and rebellion against French abuses. After having been detailed by Captain Raymond concerning the kidnapping of the general, Diatta does not impede the act. In the midst of unbridled African uprising when Diatta is asked whether he is with or against the Africans, he responds that he is with them. Diatta's hesitant yet affirmative acknowledgement of solidarity represents not only an important awareness of his victimization but also a committed act that stands in opposition to the continued allegiance of Abdelakader. The point of this comparison, then, is to demonstrate how diverse reactions to the French assimilationist policy underscore different victim positions that might ultimately suggest the availability of different subjective positions in relationship to the history of victimization. The mapping of such diverse positions consequently engenders a questioning of the victimizer's policies and enables a more thorough understanding of the complexity of reactions that may prevail in relationship to them. Moreover, this type of comparative mapping of the imperialist experience in history does not inscribe the victim in a static position in relation to victimization; it opens up new ways of thinking about the historical position of the colonial victim that might ultimately enable a more complete and open-ended spectrum of positions and responses that might elude appropriation.

A salient example of comparative subjectivities in relation to this part of France's colonial World War II history raised by *Indigènes* is that of the oppressed subject himself, in this case, and his ability to testify to imperialist victimization. Sembene's *Camp de Thiaroye* builds this very question into its composition through the character Pays, which means country, whose very presence in the film signals the desperate attempt to map imperialist victimization and to plot its future trajectory. Further, I would argue that Pays's presence represents some of the very issues central to the plotting of spaces of colonial victimization in history: the attempt to testify to the designation of a space that can be invested by the victimizing impulse and mechanism; the attempt to portray how analogous spaces of victimization are historically related; the attempt to appropriate space and designate it as a place where oppression takes place with full knowledge that even the very testimony to the space of victimization is *a priori* appropriated by the very Manichean dynamics of victimization.

The representation of the North African soldiers' devotion to the French mission in *Indigènes*, in many ways, raises the question of their capacity to testify to colonial oppression and its potential future trajectory. While it is true that the soldiers' very loyalty to the French cause is a form of testimony to the way they are mentally colonized, it is also true that this type of loyalty does not enable them, as we have seen, to speak out against the very injustices to which they are subject, particularly since doing so would undermine the representation of their devotion. In this way *Indigènes* raises Gayatri Spivak's still relevant question of whether the subaltern can speak. More accurately, it raises the question of how the subaltern can speak. In *Camp de Thiaroye* this very question is built into Sembene's representation of Pays, an African soldier who has lost the faculty of speech after his experience as a prisoner in Buchenwald. Wearing a Wehrmacht helmet as a continuous sign of Nazi oppression, Pays can only utter wordless groans, serving as the figure for what Giorgio Agamben terms "bare life," a remnant of the processes dividing life and death that gives authority to testimony: "The authority of the witness consists in his capacity to speak solely in the name of an incapacity to speak" (158). Further, Agamben argues that the figure of "bare life" resides in a no-man's land, an ambiguous geography situated on the other side of life and death, where biopolitics inhere as the sole governing spatial logic, a logic that finds subjects existing only as living dead within its sphere. In many ways Pays represents this logic in his speechless testimony to existence in a homeless homeland where colonial biopolitics establish a cartography of victimization in which Africa is no longer home and resembles more a German concentration camp.

Pays gurgles sounds of this impending massacre to fellow soldiers. Even when Corporal Diarra pours soil onto his hands and repeats that he is home in Africa, not Germany, Pays is not consoled. We learn later that there is no consolation to be had in one's "homeland," since Pays testifies to the reduction of life to "bare life" in a space of utter victimization. Throughout the film Pays attempts to testify to fellow soldiers in groans and guttural sounds, which remain unheeded. Moreover, the film intercuts images in Pays's head from newsreel footage of corpses being dumped in concentration camps. Here, as elsewhere, memory of victimization is intended to be multidirectional and relatable to the impending colonial genocide that will occur when the general is released. Yet, Pays remains the only African to understand this reality. His fellow officers ignore his grumbling protests that the general should not be released because he is lying about the soldiers' pay, and they ignore his warning that the French are coming to massacre them. Ultimately, Pays's testimony speaks volumes about the type of victimization the Africans endure.

Sembene uses Pays as a symbolic map that plots the direction of imperialist mentality and the colonial biopolitical reduction of life to bare life. The questions raised by Pays's impossible testimony, though, remain far more important to our understanding of the cartography of victimization than the testimony's content itself. Ultimately, Pays raises the question of how we might ever map victimization in such a way that its trajectory might be plotted across space and time without being lost. How can the subaltern victim speak without that speech being ignored or appropriated? Sembene's film urges us to consider how the map of imperialist victimization must be continuously conceived. It demonstrates that past victimization must be related to contemporary spaces where victimization, albeit frequently of another yet analogous form, is imminent. Moreover, the film demonstrates the necessity not only of relating representations of victimization to contemporary spaces but also of relating them to contemporary representations of victimization. In *Indigènes* Bouchareb attempts to speak in the name of victims of colonial history. His film, like *Camp de Thiaroye*, maps one aspect of colonial victimization. Yet, what the comparison of subjectivity raised by *Indigènes* and *Camp de Thiaroye* does is to suggest whether the plotting of victimization as testimony is ever relevant if the trajectory of historical victimization is not kept in mind. In other words might the map of victimization not simply be appropriated and redrawn by a victimizer, or potential victimizer, if the postcolonial cartographic process is not ongoing and understood as a relevant contemporary endeavor lodged clearly within the present moment.

While Bouchareb's film is successful in raising awareness of the history of North African soldiers in World War II France, the question must be asked about the scope of the director's larger intentions as stated earlier. Will this film be incorporated into the French classroom as one element of a pedagogical lesson on French history? Will its emphasis on this one aspect of French colonial history ultimately have an effect on the ways that the Other is viewed and treated in France?[14] Will the recent disenfranchised rioters of the *banlieue* in France ultimately relate to this generational history, inscribed as it is in the narrative of French nationalism? Will Chirac's recognition of former North African soldiers in his attention to their pensions end only as a symbolic gesture of inclusion?

While the above questions must be asked and, indeed, are seemingly posed by the film itself, they do not detract completely from Bouchareb's project. The role of a film like this in illuminating the larger history of World War II is clearly important. Its success in addressing the widespread social problems in France that are a part of its colonial heritage rests, to a great extent, on the ways its potential public sees not only the composition of French national identity but also the administrative, political, and instrumental underpinnings of that identity. Bouchareb's film demonstrates that while questions of inclusion and exclusion in the French national narrative of identity may be important, further probing of the specific policies and attitudes that underpin the ways national identity functions and is constituted in the contemporary context is necessary. Such an understanding would encompass the potential of national identity to fracture and inflict trauma that extends well beyond the formal borders of the nation's reflection.

3

Hidden Maps of Victimization

The Haunting Key to Colonial Victimization in *Caché*

In both France and Algeria a pervasive fascination with colonial history suggests a haunting at the very core of postcolonial interpretations of the national experience of colonialism.[1] With the influx of thousands of Maghrebian and, in particular, Algerian immigrants in France and the specters of French colonialism lingering in Algeria, discussion of postcolonial Franco-Maghrebian relations seems to remain inevitably linked to the colonial past.[2] Recent attempts in France, described in Benjamin Stora's *La Gangrène et l'oubli*, to situate the once repressed memory of its most important and closest colony, Algeria, confirm such a retrospective cultural gaze. Stora's use of the metaphor of the malady and the body through the notion of a phantom pain engendered by an amputated limb, the figure for the physical separation of France and Algeria at the time of independence, perceptively acknowledges the specters of colonialism within postcolonial memory as they relate to the ethnic body. Using a different metaphor, which ultimately figures similar effects of a haunting amputation, Etienne Balibar has identified 1962 independence as the watershed date for the embedding, or *interpénétration*, of Algeria in France and France in Algeria. Balibar suggests the haunting of both national territories by the phantom memories of Franco-Algerian colonial relations: "Il faut donc suggérer, au moins à titre d'allégorie numérique, que l'Algérie et la France, prises ensemble, ne font pas deux mais quelque chose comme un et demi, comme si chacun d'entre elles, dans leur addition, contribuait toujours déjà pour une part de l'autre" (We have to posit, at least for sake of numerical allegory, that Algeria and France, taken together, don't make two but something more like one and a half, as if each one of them, in their addition, always already contributed to a part of the other) (*Frontières* 76). Balibar evokes the inseparable nature of France and Algeria based upon the phantom presence of the colonial cultural body within both nations. In this way both Stora and Balibar suggest the important role the colonial body plays in the haunting of both contemporary France and Algeria.

In this chapter I turn to Michael Haneke's award-winning psychological thriller *Caché*, or *Hidden* (2005), a film that builds the very issue of a haunting victimization from the colonial era into both its form and content. Haneke's film demonstrates how cartographies of colonial victimization are frequently constructed in such a way as to establish a recurring and haunting fixation with the colonial past. This chapter will examine how the film functions as a map with symbols and keys that lead the spectator and the protagonist on a journey into the heart of a repetitive victimization from the colonial era. Haneke's film ultimately demonstrates that the desire to view and retrace the history of colonial victimization in a cartographic manner remains at the very heart of a certain postcolonial inability to see outside the recurring paradigm of victimization from colonial history. I will argue that the film demonstrates how France and Algeria remain haunted by the colonial era, victims of the intransigent hold of a colonial past that remains invisible, phantasmatic yet closely tied to the body as an index of the history of colonialism.

The film plays on what might be seen of the past and what remains occluded, and how that double nature of colonial history, its existence as a haunting trace to be visually plotted, ultimately creates a form of crippling and ongoing victimization. The film includes drawn pictures related to this colonial past, pictures that serve as clues for our attempts to plot the history of victimization narrated in the film from both a temporal and spatial perspective.[3]

In *Caché* the obsessive quest to view the underlying legacy of the history of colonial-era victimization leads to a generational cycle where the victimizer and victimized become one and the same, defined by a mutual desire to see the source of their victimization. The twist in *Caché*, though, is that the generational cycle of victimization remains only a suggestion, obfuscated and therefore difficult to address directly. This only augments the haunting character attached to it and underscores an accompanying obsessive and repetitive quality.[4] Like the analyses offered by Stora and Balibar, *Caché*, too, reveals how the body as a marker of national affiliation and the haunting presence of colonial history links France and Algeria in this cycle of victimization. Haneke's film explores the ways that spectatorship and the visualization of colonial-era victimization, a victimization tied to the national body, are related in ways that meld obsession and a retrospective gaze that quite often occludes the way the colonial era truly operates within the postcolonial period. Moreover, such obsessions with victimization frequently preclude an approach that would envision Franco-Maghrebi relations from the present, and instead cast them in a perpetual temporal context related to the colonial era.

Within contemporary manifestations of cultural memory in France, the focus on the haunting body of colonial history is evident in a flurry of commemorations and publications related to France's colonial history in Algeria. In June 1999, for instance, the French *Assemblée nationale* and Senate ordered that military archives related to the Algerian War be officially opened, thereby enabling a series of scholarly theses and monographs to reconstruct the battled cultural history of Franco-Algerian relations of more than forty years prior.[5] A number of notable books have since appeared, treating for the first time, in public-wide forum, the role of the state during France's occupation of Algeria. Raphaëlle Branche's popular book, *La Torture et l'armée pendant la guerre d'Algérie*, traces the roots of systematic torture in Algeria by the French military to torture techniques employed during the battle of Dien Bien Phu in Indochina (10–40). Meanwhile, Sylvie Thénault's work on the complicity of the French juridical system with military practices of torture appeared as *Une drôle de justice: Les magistrats dans la guerre d'Algérie*.[6] Such fascinations of the French cultural imaginary with its Algerian histories appear to be supplanting a once fervent fascination with World War II and the occupation, so famously labeled the "Syndrome de Vichy" by Rousso in 1989. Borrowing from Rousso's formulation, Anne Donadey has referred to France's attempts to process the unassimilated loss of Algeria as the "Algeria Syndrome" (215).[7] What interests me most about this specter of colonial history is the retrospective gaze that seems unable to approach Algeria or Franco-Maghrebi relations from the perspective of the present. While works related to the Algeria Syndrome are important in their endeavors to reveal the past, their focus on the tortured and forgotten body of colonial history frequently raises questions about the relevance of their subject matter to its contemporary context of publication.

Even putatively interventionist studies, such as Pierre Vidal-Naquet's *Les crimes de l'armée française: Algérie 1954–1962*, published in 1975 and reissued in 2001, and Jean-Pierre Rondeau's recent commentaries on medical experiments in his preface to the colonial documents, *Aspects véritables de la rébellion algérienne suivi de: Algérie médicale*, remain focused on colonial history, obscuring the relationship of their discourses to the present. Rondeau focuses exclusively on French culpability and its colonial legacy in a pedagogical commemoration of the past when he writes, "Demain, nos enfants oublieront, si ce n'est déjà fait" (Tomorrow, our children will forget, if they haven't already) (5). While the intent to reveal colonial torture for the posterity of the nation might be seen as an important historical endeavor, it remains focused on the phantom body of colonial history. Such an emphasis seems intent on assuring a national sense of culpability. Although the revisionist intent might be viewed as important and admirable, the result is often a contemporary focus on national definitions of this shared colonial history that reduce France to the image of torturer and Algeria to that of its victim. It is important to question why a pervasive focus on this criminal past is not brought to bear more poignantly on the state of contemporary, postcolonial Franco-Algerian relations. The tortured bodies of Rondeau's work appear frozen in the past as ethnic victims. Strict divisions of ethnic and national affiliation are thus redrawn between victim and torturer, between French and Algerian, simplifying only further what were always complex categories and ignoring contemporary realities, which find many people of Algerian heritage residing in France as French citizens and very much a part of France's national heritage.[8] Moreover, the pervasive fascination with the dead body of colonial history, such as that seen in Rondeau's work, suggests the lurking specter of a nationalist gaze and power intent on keeping its history under surveillance.[9] Ultimately, the perspective adopted in these works remains the paradigm of victimization.

This redrawing of national and ethnic divisions and haunting reappearance of colonial-era conflict are suggested in the 2001 reissue of Francis Jeanson's book *Notre Guerre*, censured one week after its publication in June of 1960 for "provocation à la désobéissance civile" (inciting civil disobedience) (Lemire 60). According to Laurent Lemire's review of the text in *Le Nouvel Observateur*, the reissue of Jeanson's text exemplifies a cultural shift from repression to obsession with the complex and blurred boundaries of the past in France's relationship to its Algerian histories (60). In his work Jeanson, a former French resistance fighter during the Algerian War, launches a humanist attack on colonialism that, reissued, recalls Phillipe Labro's 1967 novel on the Algerian War, *Des feux mal éteints*. The smoldering nature of colonial history in the title of Labro's novel was viewed as a fitting heading for *Le Nouvel Observateur*'s special issue on the Algerian War, dealing with the French torture of Algerian citizens during that period (Lemire 60–63). Yet, the question remains as to whether these fires really are smoldering in the postcolonial period and whether the memorabilia of the colonial era suggests a retreat of consciousness into the haunting aura of colonial memories with no real regard for the ways that national culpability might amount to nothing more than another national obsession.

Lemire's article treating the suppressed nature of French torture announces that "la vérité est enfin connue. Accablante" (the truth is finally known. Damning), suggesting that something was hidden by another generation, another group, or perhaps at best, was finally furrowed out by postcolonial consciousness stupefied by its own epiphany (60). Statements such as this suggest a haunting sense of culpability related to the Algerian War lingering within the French nation.[10] Yet, the relationship of this disclosed "truth" to contemporary postcolonial Franco-Maghrebian relations is obfuscated by a focus on strict national and ethnic divisions and their nostalgic replay. The photo accompanying the text, for instance, portrays French military operations in Kabylia in 1955, showing a standing armed French soldier lording over two unarmed fellahs prostrate on the ground. The article attempts to relate this image to a subsequent photo on the next page portraying the Nanterre *bidonville*, or shantytown, such as that of Azouz Begag's *Le Gone du Chaâba*, where many migrant Maghrebians first lived upon their arrival in France, thus gesturing toward a chronology of postcolonial diaspora.[11] These images, however, like many of their kind treating the colonial era, trade on a *noir* aesthetics depicting faded black-and-white stills of victim and perpetrator frozen in a timeless past. A recent issue of the popular French magazine *Le Point* also employs such aesthetics, its cover photo featuring a turbaned man holding a child outside of a wartime encampment. Titled "Guerre d'Algérie: Ce qu'on a *Caché*" (The Algerian War: What was *Hidden*), the issue keeps with the recurring thematic notion in French national memory of something that has been actively hidden by an impersonal, collective party. This pervasive reappearance of ethnic victims in *noir* aesthetics seems more intent on imbuing the French nation with a sense of culpability than on reorienting Franco-Maghrebian relations toward the postcolonial era.

The term "*noir* aesthetics" derives from Manthia Diawara's reading of the *noir* aesthetics of filmmaking. Diawara argues convincingly that the use of light on dark in film *noir* produced blackness as an immoral character flaw, bringing that "darkness" visibly to light. Diawara's assertion of the moral and racialized quality of the *noir* image can bring insight to the photographic aesthetics one finds in many returning images of colonial Algeria today. With their gazes turned back onto France, the victims and landscapes of colonial-era Algeria are positioned to reverse the immoral "shot code" of Algerian victims onto the French nation. In other words the nostalgia and retrospective gaze found in many works that focus on France's Algerian histories, although not necessarily always strictly cast in *noir*, nonetheless evince a certain concern with the revelation of a dark and immoral past lurking within the French nation, a past frequently signaled through the turn to an "ethnic" or ethnicized body of an Algerian. Moreover, the play of light on dark discussed by Diawara is similar to what one might term a postcolonial "illumination effect," whereby the French nation is illuminated by the return of the "dark," "immoral" side of its enlightenment and colonial histories. I refer to Diawara's conception of *noir* aesthetics in relationship to a postcolonial ethics here because of the attempt to reveal or bring to light the culpability hidden within the nation through a return of a colonial repressed. The implicit racialized quality intended by Diawara is important in the postcolonial context where Algerians and ethnic difference are signifiers of alterity that frequently references French colonial history and its ethical position today. Yet, I want to emphasize that this return of the colonial repressed is not necessarily, as Haneke's film demonstrates so well, a salutary event. When the return of the colonial repressed is based upon the paradigm of victimization, the ensuing culpability and paralysis of cultural relations that can often occur, does not lead to any real confrontation with the legacy of colonial history. On the contrary, quite often it suggests a replay of colonial-era scenes of terror cast within the postcolonial context.

In many ways *Caché* engages the very concept of Diawara's *noir* aesthetics in relationship to colonial objectification and the designation and recognition of an inherent criminal history related to race. The film plays on the very trope of victimization and on the returning and returned gaze of victim and victimizer. Set in contemporary Paris, the film focuses on a typical bourgeois family. Georges, the paternal figurehead, is the host of a popular television show on the lives of seminal French novelists, akin to the real life Bernard Pivot. He begins to receive videotapes of the family apartment and its comings and goings accompanied by childlike drawings of stick figures in red. The intrigue of the film really begins with the arrival of the first tape. The tape's first shot is, indeed, footage from the camera pointed at Georges's apartment building that we view along with Georges and his wife. The tape simply runs as a still showing the outside of the apartment and any movement that occurs.[12] What is most disturbing for Georges is the gaze without a face that he discerns in these tapes. The tape, though, is accompanied by the childlike drawing of a round nondescript face, seemingly vomiting blood. While watching the clip, Georges remembers the image of a young boy, which appears to the viewer in a flash sequence, with blood covering part of his chin and face, similar to the drawing. We later learn that this was an Algerian boy who lived with Georges's family when he was young. What we do not understand at this point is that the image is a flashback of Majid, son of an Algerian family that worked for Georges's family and its estate. The image flashes for a second as George replays the video footage of his family being watched, but the image is only a flashback from Georges's past that he imagines. In this way the film's opening scene establishes the equation between victimization and a returning yet unseen gaze from the past. Although the image is clearly from Georges's past, he tells his wife that he has no understanding of the tape or its meaning.

As the film progresses and other tapes and similar drawings arrive, we follow Georges's growing consciousness of the meaning and context of the tapes. We learn, for instance, that in the 1960s an Algerian family worked for Georges's family. The dates turn out to be quite significant since we learn that Majid's parents were among the casualties of the 17 October 1961 Paris massacre. On this date a peaceful demonstration took place in Paris with thirty thousand unarmed Algerians protesting conditions, such as a curfew, which had been imposed upon them by the French government during the Algerian War. The protest was met with violent suppression by Parisian police prefect Maurice Papon. Majid's parents were among those Algerians who disappeared. Orphaned, Majid found himself alone, and George's family considered adopting the boy. Out of jealousy and fear of Majid, Georges began to invent stories about the orphan, suggesting that he was ill, and eventually concocting a scheme to assure that the family would not carry out the adoption. He told Majid to kill the family's rooster, and Majid cut off the rooster's head with an axe, covering him with blood. When Georges subsequently claimed that Majid had done this to scare him, Majid was sent away to an orphanage. Although no explanation is given as to the identity of the tape's sender, the film plays on this story and its symbolism and the historical context of French colonialism to illustrate the relationship between an occluded and unresolved colonial history, spectatorship, and the cycle of postcolonial victimization.

Before considering the important symbolism of this family saga in detail, some contextualization is in order. The very role of the French family and its act of orphaning the Algerian boy is important to a full understanding of the film and its relationship to colonial history. Although the context for this story from 17 October 1961 could appear to be a simple narrative device to propel the plot, I would like to argue that it is central to the film's larger narrative concerning victimization, colonial history, and postcolonial haunting. The reference to 17 October 1961 is not without a heavy history within the French context. During the height of the Algerian War and on the eve of Algerian independence in late August 1961, the FLN had resumed bombings against the French police. During that time eleven police were killed and others were injured in Paris and its suburbs. According to historian Jean-Luc Einaudi, "These bombings had the effect of spreading fear throughout the ranks of the Paris police, but also for increasing the desire for revenge and hate against the whole of the community. During the whole of September, the Algerian population was severely repressed. In practice, this massive repression was based on physical appearance" (76). During the month of September, Algerians, and any other "ethnic" population that resembled an Algerian, were subject to raids and frequent arrests at work; some were arrested and thrown into the Seine with their hands tied behind their backs. This oppression worsened, and on 5 October 1961 Maurice Papon announced the introduction of a curfew from 8:30 p.m. to 5:30 a.m. affecting "Algerian Muslim workers," "French Muslims," and "French Muslims of Algeria" in Paris and its suburbs. Of course, despite Papon's terminology, the one hundred fifty thousand Algerians living in Paris at that time officially were considered French. After the introduction of this curfew, the French federation of the FLN called upon the Algerian population in Paris and beyond to demonstrate peacefully against the measure, which was being considered a form of institutionalized racism on the part of the state. Nearly thirty thousand Algerians protested. Papon mobilized nearly seven thousand police officers and other riot police to block the demonstration, arresting more than eleven thousand people. Many of those arrested were rounded up and transported by buses to internment centers used under Vichy, such as the Parc des Expositions. According to Einaudi systematic torture took place within the detainment center, and many Algerians were badly injured and killed. The police shot at crowds, killing Algerians near the Neuilly bridge, which separates Paris from the suburbs, and near Notre Dame on the Saint Michel bridge, near the center of Paris and the Prefecture of Police. Hundreds were estimated dead, though counted simply as missing, much like the parents of Majid in *Caché*. Bodies were thrown into the Seine, and numerous unidentified bodies continued to surface days later.

In order to understand fully the depth of this event it is important to recall that many former members of the police forces in place during the World War II Vichy regime that had collaborated with the Gestapo to detain and deport Jews were still serving under Papon in 1961. Many officers suspended during the liberation for extreme forms of collaborationism were later reinstated. Indeed, Papon himself was tried for crimes against humanity in his collaborationist role in the deportation of over fifteen hundred Jews from 1942 to 1944. During the Papon trial some forty years later in 1997 and 1998, left-wing minister Jean-Pierre Chevènement ordered the opening of parts of the archives concerning this period that had been officially closed until then. The Mandelken report, based on these archives, registered thirty-two Algerians dead. Einaudi then contested this figure in an op-ed published in *Le Monde*. Numerous contested figures emerged in the aftermath, with Einaudi counting as many as over two hundred victims. The accurate death toll still remains largely unknown today. In 1998 the French government acknowledged that the massacre occurred and that forty people died. Then, in 2001, the city of Paris officially acknowledged the event, unveiling a commemorative plaque placed near the Saint Michel bridge. Socialist prime minister Lionel Jospin spoke openly about the "tragic events" but refused to elaborate on the responsibility for them. To this day there have been no prosecutions related to the massacres given that they fell under amnesty for crimes committed during the Algerian War. In many ways we might say that the event has remained hidden as a national trauma, a guilty spot partially revealed and monumentalized within French culture.

Although popular representations of the massacre, such as the French documentary *Nuit noire, 17 octobre 1961* and Leïla Sebbar's novel *La Seine était rouge*, have begun to emerge, the massacre has remained largely hidden for many years. What is critical about this cultural obfuscation, and what highlights its importance for its inclusion in Haneke's film, is the way that the legacy of an un-integrated event of these proportions from colonial history returns, partially, to bother, indeed to haunt, the French national scene.

In *Caché* the event remains a historical trace, mentioned but classified rather quickly by Georges when he finally reveals Majid's personal history and his own wrongdoing as a child to his wife much later. Georges references the massacre in much the same way that it appears on the Saint Michel bridge plaque, as an event that is factual and little more, part of history that remains in the past, acknowledged but unimportant with respect to the current situation. However, the very history of the relationship between Majid and Georges suggests that the legacy of the event remains a much more profound and disturbing narrative of national and, I will argue below, international proportions; it returns with a vengeance to structure the very film and the evolution of its narrative. Moreover, it reveals how a continuing form of postcolonial victimization remains linked to that event.

The drawings that Georges receives serve as a key that leads him to ponder the relationship between the way his own family is being victimized through an unknown gaze and his own victimization of Majid years earlier.[13] The red of the drawing recalls the blood that covered Majid, but it also symbolically references the blood of 17 October 1961 and the blood of a much larger story of familial belonging. The film widens the personal parameters of Georges's story to national dimensions through its related symbolism of the rooster, blood, narratives of illness, decapitation, violence, and ultimately a refused adoption. Georges's recall of the stories he told about Majid to have him rejected from the family household, stories of illness, is not uncommon to colonial history. One might recall Ferdinand Céline's *Voyage au bout de la nuit*, or Joseph Conrad's *Heart of Darkness*, where illness and narrative are often equated with an indigenous and undesirable colonial subject. Georges's rejection of Majid from the family estate, although seemingly a simple childhood story, is cast in symbolic terms that suggest a French national rejection of Algeria.

Georges's family owns an estate, a stereotypical French country manor with ties to the land. We see the estate for the first time in one of the videotapes that arrives. It, too, is simply shot as a still in real time. Coupled with this stereotypical emblem of French national identity is the rooster itself. As a national emblem for France, the *Coq Gaulois*, or Gallic Rooster, is a symbol for the French because of its Latin roots, *gallus* meaning Gaul and rooster. Although the rooster has taken on different meanings throughout French history, alternately adorning flags during the Revolution and those of the July Monarchy and Second Republic, it has long been associated with the French nation and with the symbol of liberty. Since roughly 1848 the rooster has been on the seal of the Republic, adorning Liberty. Further, for the purposes of the present discussion, it is important to remember that the July Monarchy of 1830 initiated active colonization in Algeria. Majid's massacre of the rooster on the family estate with an axe, then, is a highly symbolic gesture. The fact that Georges sets him up to do this only to have Majid ultimately rejected by his family for this act, serves as a microcosmic reference to colonial history and the colonial Algerian relationship to the French nation. The French colonizing forces ultimately created a situation of dependency in Algeria, and in other colonies, the outcome of which could be none other than a violent severing. After, the desired union with the French nation that had become part of the legacy of relations between the two nations was refused by the French.[14] In fact, that desire continues to be rejected by right-wing sentiment that calls for the expulsion of Algerian and other immigrants today. The blood from the rooster, the national mess that is a fallout of the colonial relationship, not only serves to recall the generational blood that covers Majid for the "sins" of his parents who simply wished to be a part of the French nation with all its liberties on 17 October 1961, but it also becomes an indelible spot of blame that will not allow him to enter into union with the French nation through a symbolic adoption.[15] In many ways it marks the victim as the victimizer of the French nation, the cause of its problems. Georges, too, adopts this stance with Majid, who he later encounters. He even awakens one night from a dream in which he envisions the young Majid killing the rooster and then threatening him with the axe. Once Georges suspects Majid of sending the tapes and of threatening his family, he becomes fixated on this history, and on protecting his family. The symbolism of his protectionism points to a larger national proprietary attitude, a fear of contamination from the colonial Other and a return that recalls the stories of illness Georges once told about Majid. Moreover, this proprietary attitude is underscored when Georges meets Majid in his apartment.

This victimization turns into a vicious cycle, one which leads Georges to Majid's apartment after a tape arrives showing a street sign, Avenue Lenin, and the dimly lit hallway of an HLM. The reference to Lenin, where Majid lives, underscores the irony of the failure of the French Communist Party in its relationship to the legacy of colonial history, immigration, and assimilation of postcolonial minorities in France. But the reference is not necessarily only incriminating. It also recalls what is popularly referred to in France as "l'Affaire de la station de métro Charonne" (the Charonne metro station incident) on 8 February 1962. Viewed as a follow-up to the October 17 massacre, the Charonne incident represented another episode of violent police oppression. This time, the oppression was wielded primarily against the French Communist Party, which had organized a protest on that date in favor of Algerian independence. Numerous French Communist Party members were killed in the police violence.[16] Georges's attempt to locate Avenue Lenin on a Parisian map, and his subsequent trip to that place, remaps the history of victimization that began in Paris on October 17 and continued throughout the city. In many ways we might say that the film establishes a symbolic cartography of the diaspora of colonial victimization in Paris through these references and the retracing of the route to Majid's apartment near Avenue Lenin.

Although Majid claims to have no knowledge of the tapes nor of the drawing, he is interested in talking to Georges face to face when he arrives. Majid is surprised that Georges did not take over the family estate, a fact he knows from having seen the latter on television, and when threatened concerning the tapes remarks, "What would one not do to protect what is one's own." The reference emphasizes Majid's placement on the periphery of French society. He lives in an HLM building of the Paris suburbs, and the implication is that he has lived a life on the French borders ever since his rejection by Georges's family. The French family saga, the underpinnings of bourgeois society and class distinction, becomes the icon of a much larger narrative concerning the composition of French national identity and belonging, one ultimately rooted in the symbolic blood of the massacred rooster. As if to underscore this fact, the scene following Georges's departure shows Majid weeping. Moreover, to suggest further the symbolic nature of a French national narrative of belonging and proximity, Majid remarks that he has seen Georges on television talking to French authors face to face. Here, the concept of a distinct national narrative permitting union and dialogue with certain types of people is in play. Majid points out that if Georges had seen Majid on the street, he would most likely have continued to walk past with no acknowledgement of his existence. At the same time the scene is a clear indictment of Majid's focus on the way he was victimized or excluded in the past.

However, what is perhaps most interesting about this scene in Majid's apartment is not necessarily the threat and its consequences but the fact that a tape arrives almost immediately after Georges's visit, which shows the entire scene. This return of the saga of victimization underscores the way that the mimetic nature of postcolonial victimization plays itself out as a haunting repetition of the past. Georges, and indeed we as spectators, cannot see outside the paradigm of victimization within the film. Subject to its scenes, we are also subject to their replay. In this way Haneke's film underscores the difficulty of establishing a visual perspective outside the paradigm of colonial history and its return when victimization remains the central visual and thematic perspective of organization. Moreover, the desire to see the author of this victimization plays into this very cycle itself. Georges himself is quick to imagine that Majid has created this entire scenario and that it is he who has sent the tapes. Here, again, the unknown quality of the returning gaze of a long history of victimization rooted in the colonial era is what disturbs and ultimately exacerbates the cycle of victimization itself.

Although scenes of victimization are replayed within the film, one capital scene cannot be confronted directly, and it is ultimately this type of victimization as a capital scene — multidirectional in its historical reference — that, kept in the dark, returns us back to the starting point of the very history of victimization. Upon receiving the tape of himself and Majid, Georges returns to Majid's apartment. Here, Majid closes the door admitting he is glad Georges came since he wanted him to see his act. He then promptly draws a knife across his throat in suicide as Georges watches aghast. It is within this scene that the cartography of victimization is completed. Georges has become victim of the ultimate victim. Moreover, Majid's act might be said to constitute the ultimate form of victimization, since the reciprocation of victimization cannot take place and Georges is left with the haunting vision. We might say that Majid's suicide, his self-victimization, encapsulates the inevitability of the cycle of violence, the circularity of a story that replays itself over and over. Moreover, this scene never returns in videotape. It is as if the founding scene of severing and victimization at the heart of the problem cannot be represented in its entirety and can only live on, as we shall see below, as a haunting scene reiterated generationally.

In addition, Majid's specific act of slitting his throat ties together numerous historical references in the film. First, the act recalls the drawings that Georges receives and establishes a resonance with the severed throat of the rooster, the symbol for the French nation.

Further drawn, the act also aligns with the blood of the October 17 massacre, where impossible union was the very cause for a symbolic orphaning of Algerian immigrants and French citizens of Algerian origin. The fact that Majid slits his throat suggests a generational transfer of this traumatic act of national orphaning, especially since his parents were amongst those victims of 1961. The act holds wider international symbolic resonances still, though, since it embodies the very act of the *égorgeur*, or "throat slitter," of the Algerian War as well as of contemporary Algeria.

During the Algerian War the French practice of torture was revealed by Benoist Rey's controversial book *Les Égorgeurs*, published by Editions de Minuit in 1961 and immediately censured by the French government. The book serves as a chronicle of French Army practices during the war and reveals the commonplace tactic of cutting throats to subdue the Algerian population. Rey writes, "Chacun sait que les prisonniers sont 'consommables,' c'est-à-dire qu'il faut les égorger ou les tuer d'une manière quelconque avant de rentrer au camp" (Everyone knows that the prisoners are "expendable," that is to say, that they must have their throats cut or be killed in a similar manner before we return to camp) (79). According to Rey this practice was a common form of terrorism intended to instill fear in others, in a word, to victimize them through a campaign of physical and visual terrorism. Rey's work, although censured in 1961, has received renewed interest and in 1999 received the Grand Prix "Ni Dieu ni Maître" in France. It was subsequently reedited in 2000 by Editions du Monde Libertaire. Although this is not the place to examine how Rey's work participates in the larger culture of the Algeria Syndrome outlined at the outset of this chapter, it suffices to say that the return to the site of colonial torture and victimization that has been long denied a place of memory in France is a part of this project.

However, the book, even in its newly released form, remains focused on colonial victimization in Algeria, and in many ways Haneke's film, with its focus on the colonial era and a reciprocal form of victimization between French and Algerians, addresses this problematic. Majid's act, though a clear visual marker of colonial-era victimization in Algeria, can be seen as an embodiment of contemporary terrorism by Algerian fundamentalists, also known as *égorgeurs*, who cut the throats of victims too aligned with Western values. These terrorists are known for their stealth acts, a certain invisible ninja quality. In many ways Majid's act, as a form of mimetic victimization rooted in colonial era bloodshed and exclusion, points outwardly toward that other form of terrorism in Algeria so closely related to French colonial terror.

The terrorism of contemporary *égorgeurs* in Algeria functions in much the same way that Majid's act functions in the film; it replays scenes of French victimization as a founding reference point, one that signals the mimetic nature of colonial-era victimization replayed within the postcolonial context. In many ways contemporary terrorists in Algeria are simply replaying the Algerian War as a civil war, cutting throats of victims in a campaign of terror and exclusion where the West and its Other are not allowed to cohabit.[17] The fundamentalist nature of such terrorism establishes the polarity between Algeria and its Other, a polarity similar to that of the colonial era. Majid's act embodies visually the centrality of this mimetic victimization, one form of terrorism simply replacing another from the colonial era. In this way Haneke's film also functions as a commentary on the way that the historical map of victimization is drawn full circle.

Nowhere in the film, perhaps, is this more evident than in the final scene, when the camera films the school Georges's son attends. We notice Majid's son and Georges's son talking together. While the implication might be that the two conspired together in creating and sending the videotapes, the film leaves the mystery unresolved. However, pointing to a generational linking of the history we have come to witness, the film ends on spectatorial implication in the cyclical nature of colonial-era victimization. We seek a resolution to the problem of victimization, a way of placing it within this history so rooted in the colonial era. However, the film demonstrates that when colonial-era victimization remains central to this postcolonial narrative, any attempt to return to a founding answer to the cyclical nature of victimization within the postcolonial context simply perpetuates the cycle.[18] It leads us back in time to recall the very scenes of victimization for further clues that would resolve the identity of victim and victimizer. The film's ambiguous and suggestive ending, based as it is on a generational narrative, haunts because it leaves the spectator to contemplate this history. However, it is just such a contemplation that ultimately speaks to the way that contemporary manifestations of cultural memory in France remain rooted in a colonial lexicon.

Works such as that by Benoist Rey and those cited at the outset of this chapter participate in a cultural cult or fascination with colonial-era victimization. They are psychological thrillers, much like Haneke's film, not so much because their focus remains the culprit, but because they play on the dark and haunting nature of historical victimization buried within the postcolonial context. In *Caché* much of this intrigue might be attributed to the film's play on darkness and light as both a formal and thematic device. Haneke's film plays on a form of *noir* aesthetics on several occasions, as if to articulate the very nature of the return of colonial-era victimization and culpability in postcolonial France. Frequently, Georges is filmed in dark rooms or corridors where the return of colonial-era victimization comes to light. One of the first instances of this occurs during a dream sequence. Asleep in a dark room, Georges dreams of Majid coming toward him with the axe he has used to decapitate the rooster. The dream sequence takes place on a bright and sunny day in the French countryside. It is interrupted when Georges awakens in the dark reality of his modern bedroom. Not only does this play of light on darkness suggest a haunting by the return of the colonial repressed, symbolically, it also suggests how the movement into French modernity was accompanied by a repression of the site of colonial-era victimization. Such a movement corresponds to the placement of postcolonial minorities on the peripheral areas of French metropolitan centers. The second salient example of this play on darkness can be seen when Georges enters the HLM where Majid lives. The corridor is dimly lit, and poor light flickers as Georges walks through the hallway leading to Majid's apartment. When Georges enters the apartment, he is greeted by Majid in bright light. Here, again, the contrast of lighting plays on the return of the colonial era. The third significant instance of *noir* aesthetics is seen upon Georges's return from Majid's apartment after the latter has committed suicide. Georges enters his house quietly and surreptitiously draws the curtains of the windows. He calls his wife and informs her that the guests should leave and that she should come talk to him in the darkened bedroom. When she arrives he informs her of Majid's suicide. The scenes of victimization are illuminated here in stark contrast to the blunted darkness of their prelude and aftermath. Such a contrast suggests the lurking of an immoral quality, a hidden past that flashes up only to be returned to darkness. Yet, most importantly, these scenes are informed by the very cyclical and repetitive vision of a recurring victimization.

Haneke's film provides an important commentary on this interplay. Although the film clearly indicts the failure of postcolonial memory to address the legacy of colonialism, and in particular, the events of 1961, it also showcases the vicissitudes of a form of memory focused on colonial-era victimization. The images and wounds of colonial-era history, when serving as the prism through which postcolonial relations are viewed, often only serve to fuel a repetitive vision of terror. The responsibility of seeing postcolonial relations outside such a paradigm of colonial victimization remains that of both victim and victimizer. Indeed, as Haneke's film shows, the border separating these two, particularly with respect to the relationship between French and Algerians, is never clearly demarcated, and victim and victimizer are quite frequently one and the same. In many ways this remains the reason that the centrality of the victim paradigm is so important in *Caché*; it reveals how the urge to identify the victim or victimizer within the context of the legacy of colonial history remains a dangerous gesture, one which returns us to a repeating and generationally transferred history. The point underscored by the film is not that we should neglect the history of imperialism, but that our understanding of it as a narrative opposing polar moral characteristics is essentially mistaken.

The Algeria Syndrome might be best understood not merely as an obsessive focus on the history of Franco-Algerian colonial relations but as a national obsession with victimization and culpability. In the case of France the extremes of culpability or repression with regard to the history of colonialism, such as those seen in *Caché*, are predicated on the paradigm of victimization. The trauma of confronting a nation's victimizing history or the obsessive focus on its culpability both constitute gestures firmly rooted in the cause of the nation and in its composition. In contemporary Algeria it is clear that a focus on colonial victimization by the French has engendered a certain replication of victimization and terrorism within the postcolonial period by some fundamentalist factions. In the case of both France and Algeria victimization remains central to the nationalist vision of the colonial era, and it obscures the postcolonial gaze from seeing anything but a mimetic view of colonial-era history.

Caché creates a key to the history of colonial-era victimization that structures Franco-Maghrebi relations. The film leads its protagonist and its viewer to reconstruct a history of colonial-era victimization, replete with the severed body that would symbolically unite France and Algeria. In so doing it points to the ways that France and Algeria remain linked in their relationship to colonial history. Colonial-era narratives and images replay within the postcolonial period with different actors and modified scripts. However, the story remains essentially the same, and the vision is one of extreme terror and ultimate victimization. *Caché* functions much like the mapping process itself. It plots sites and leads us from one geographically and historically significant space of victimization to another. Its play on the hidden or obfuscated quality of colonial-era victimization tempts us to seek final answers that would enable us to reconstruct fully the history and legacy of culpability. The film functions as a commentary on the very act of plotting or mapping spaces (and their histories) of colonial-era victimization. It maps the legacy of 17 October 1961 as well as the history of French colonialism in Algeria and Algerian immigration in France through specific images that embody the unplotted images of the legacy of victimization from those periods. However, as the film demonstrates, a return to such terrain, without a full understanding of the consequences of reconstructing its history, runs the risk of simply reiterating the cycle of victimization and its images of terror. Within the postcolonial context, this risk is dangerous since the mimetic nature of terror, one image and act simply mocking another across space and time, establishes a map where terror remains key to our understanding of geopolitics, and the victim's position becomes the cipher through which nations live and die.

4

Creating an Old Maghreb

Beur Cinema and East-West Polarities

Since the appearance of a cinema produced by children of North African immigrants in France in the early 1980s, debates about integration and assimilation of France's minority populations have alternately receded only to reappear during periods of political strength shown by France's right-wing political constituencies. France's recent riots brought renewed attention to debates about whether its minority populations of North African origin and heritage were well assimilated into the fabric of the nation. Framing those riots and the corresponding discussions about cultural assimilation were larger discourses on relationships between the West and the Arab world, influenced most recently by 9/11, the "war on terrorism" in Afghanistan and Iraq, and the oil crisis. In France divergent opinions continue to prevail about whether issues of socio-cultural assimilation raised by *beur* filmmakers beginning in the early 1980s have been fully resolved. Many of those early films, such as Mehdi Charef's *Le Thé au harem d'Archimède*, the title itself revealing a symbolic attachment to underlying issues of physical displacement and spatial relations, were concerned with "reframing difference" and positing the question of the place and cultural identity of France's *beur* populations within the French nation (Tarr, *Reframing* 8–15). These films now constitute a genre of cinema, categorized by the terms *beur* or, sometimes, *banlieue* cinema, and many have achieved mainstream popularity for their humorous and popular treatments of excluded ethnic minorities in France.[1]

My interest in this chapter resides not in consolidating the genre as an important form of social commentary (Tarr, *Reframing* 3), nor in rehearsing its corresponding message about the multicultural identity of *beur* children in relationship to French national identity (Hargreaves; Higbee). As a genre, *beur* cinema, or *cinéma de banlieu*, has become acknowledged, if nonetheless frequently overlooked, as an integral corpus contributing to wider conceptions of European cinema (Ezra, *European Cinema* 290–98).[2] In this chapter I examine the way that important Francophone *beur* films that are now acknowledged to be part of the wider canon turn to victimization as an important trope. I am interested in the ways that the representation of the *beur* or *beurette*'s path to cultural emancipation or social integration within France is frequently dependent upon a polarity between East and West and is informed in great part by the evocation of the East rooted in colonial tropes and imagery. The reinscription of this aged construction, as Edward Said demonstrates, has been a focal point in the relationship between culture and imperialism, one that has enabled the West to view its "Other" as a simultaneously symbiotic and hostile reflection (*Culture*). If *beur* cinema often seeks to situate its *beur* characters in a hybrid position between the East and West to expose better the dilemmas of cultural assimilation and French patterns of exclusion and racism, such representations frequently play upon the conception of North Africa as an "old" continent distanced from the West and its modernity, both culturally and temporally. The image of the "old" here does not connote an ideal or utopian place removed from the problems of the Western world either; it refers more to the stereotypes of backward nations with retrograde views on cultural and social relations. Of course, frequently, these representations of an "old" Algeria, characterized by its alignment with the colonial era, are intended as oppositional representations designed to show how Algerian immigrants were perceived by the French. However, I would also like to point out how the adoption of that perspective and the choice to represent Algeria and Algerians in that way enables the representation of the *beur* or *beurette* subject's integration into French culture and distancing from his or her parents.

The postcolonial identifications of socio-cultural dilemmas related to assimilation and racism have provided *beur* films with the characterization as resistant and oppositional representations. They are often characterized as deploying "an appeal for social change" (Bloom 51), a "hybrid" oppositional stance (Hargreaves and McKinney), and an aesthetics of the inhospitable world of the housing projects (Fahdel 142). Patricia Geesey underscores the "spatial aspect" of the quest "for the creation of a new concept of citizenship and belonging for France's increasingly diverse community" (205). Geesey points out that the sense of belonging in French culture that *beur* characters seek is often predicated upon a literal and symbolic appropriation of space and culture (205). Teshome H. Gabriel and Hamid Naficy propose that transnational experiences, such as those of *beur* filmmakers, translated into cinema in the forms of third cinema and exilic cinema, respectively, find their opposition in that they establish a new political landscape not defined in relationship to a colonial dominant. In many ways the spatial appropriation noted by Geesey is inherent in the staking out of the new political space that Gabriel and Naficy identify. While it is difficult to disagree with the innovative and revisionist qualities attributed to *beur* cinema, it is also important to note how the metropolitan spatial investment of these films is often dependent upon the trope of Maghrebi characters and spaces in France as backward and retrograde, distanced from modernity and aligned more closely with the stereotype of an "old" colonial-era

Maghreb.[3] My concern with this representational pattern is in the creation of a spatially and temporally distant cultural image of the Maghreb, opposed to Western progress, that draws upon existing conceptions and resonances of stereotypes about Arabs, particularly in the wake of 9/11 and the recent civil unrest of France's riots. While I would be reticent to state that such representations simply reinforce stereotypes of North Africans as terrorists, I would point out that they do seem to play on an opposition where entrance into the West, or France in this case, depends upon just such an opposition between West and East. The *beur*'s success and liberation in the West is dependent, in other words, upon a duality that opposes the West and a retrograde image of North Africa.[4] Although this duality is, in great measure, required by the West, the choice of representing it this way suggests that there is no other choice and that successful integration into the West remains the only path to redemption.

In some ways such representations can be understood to reproduce Samuel Huntington's infamous "clash of civilizations," opposing the West to the East, as well as to Islam. Huntington's work has received renewed attention in the wake of 9/11, and it was used as a viable explanation for civil tensions during the French riots of 2005 in a *New York Times* article by Craig Smith. Of course there is good reason to suspect a real clash of the West and the Arab world in France. Figures published in 2000 suggest that 63 percent of the French feel that there are too many Arabs living in France (Kédadouche 65). For this reason it is important to examine how these films, although important endeavors in their portrayal of diaspora, might also inadvertently replicate a colonial-era mentality that has gained increasing capital as of late. My interest here resides in exploring how the representations of Algeria found in important *beur* films often distance it from France and align it with a colonial temporality. In many ways this distancing actually elides the real clash of civilizations that has taken place in France, most recently during the riots of 2005, since it depicts France and North Africa inhabiting the same material space yet often distanced in spatial, temporal, and cultural terms.[5]

In this chapter I will focus on three popular films by important *beur* filmmakers, *Le Gone du Chaâba* by Azouz Begag and Christophe Ruggia, *Samia* by Soraya Nini and Philippe Faucon, and *L'Autre monde* by Merzak Allouache, all of which inscribe, in different symbolic ways, the Maghreb and certain Maghrebian characters in alignment with a perpetual colonial space. In their endeavors to present the cultural dilemmas facing *beur* characters in their transnational experiences of and between France and the Maghreb, these films all attempt to position the *beur* character as a subject caught between the modernity of the West and a colonial-era image of the Maghreb. They also showcase the victimization of North African immigrants and their children. These films frequently can be understood as participating in the social realist mode. They attempt to literally map the place of the *beur* subject and some, like Begag and Ruggia's *Le Gone du Chaâba*, can be seen as period pieces that focus on the victimization of North African immigrants in the post–World War II era. The return to the colonial era and its immediate aftermath, inclusive of the attendant representations of victimization faced by North African immigrants and their children in France, is often viewed as an important and resistant form of postcolonial representation. At their best, such films attempt to revise conceptions of the French nation and of its underlying assumptions about French national identity and the role of Maghrebian immigrants within its structure.[6] Clearly, such representations are important, but the aim of this chapter, in keeping with the larger line of questioning in this book, is to ask a difficult question of such representations — namely, are there ways in which the return to colonial-era history within the age of terror might actually subvert the resistant or oppositional nature of such endeavors? This is particularly to the point given the current civil warfare in Algeria and unrest in the Maghreb since retrograde representations of a Maghrebian subject or of the Maghreb might easily align with the stereotypes and images opposing West and East produced by the recent history of terrorism there. In a larger sense, though, I am interested in how these films align the

Maghreb with its colonial image and temporality. In other words how might we see that these films represent the Maghreb as a place caught in the time of colonialism and, in a sense, doomed to repeat the images, problems, and stereotypes of a national conglomerate lagging behind the modernity of the West so germane to the colonial and neocolonial worldview? In the films I examine in this chapter, the emancipation or liberation of the *beur* subject, at times, is played off against images of Algeria trapped in a temporally frozen quasi-colonial archive. Liberation of the *beur* character frequently depends upon the depiction of "Arab" space as a cloistered, repetitive, and culturally stagnant place, and upon "Western" space as a liberatory and progressive ideal. It is the creation of this binary opposition of Western and Arab space that I will examine in filmic narratives of the *beur* subject's cultural emancipation.[7]

Azouz Begag and Christophe Ruggia have produced, to date, the most popular *beur* film of the Francophone world. Their 1997 adaptation of Begag's popular autobiographical novel *Le Gone du Chaâba* can be understood as a period piece in the social realist mode. It returns to the immediate post–Algerian War period when masses of North African immigrants sought refuge and material stability in France. The film's opening shot sequence sets the tone for the way images of an "old" Algeria are created and played off against the more progressive vision of Western-French perspective. This progression and spatial perspective of the film symbolically play into the story of the cultural integration of Omar, the film's young protagonist and narrator.

The scene begins in the Chaâba, the Arabic term for a *bidonville*, or shantytown. Shantytowns housed numerous early Maghrebian immigrants in France during the 1960s and were transitional habitations made of cardboard and natural materials. Their placement on the peripheries of metropolitan France made them predecessors to today's HLM. The opening shot of the film begins with a close-up of Omar's parents' preparations for the day. While the screen informs us that we are in France in 1965, the radio also establishes the film's historical context through its broadcast of the three-year anniversary celebrations of official Algerian independence from French colonialism. While the radio establishes the spatial distinction between France and Algeria, the film's treatment of the spatial positioning of the Chaâba and of Omar's father, Bouzid, serves to confuse the actual spatial placement of the Algerian immigrant community while establishing their position as distant and removed from France. This is so because the Chaâba gives every appearance of an Algerian community completely removed from French culture and topography. The film's depiction of the isolation of the Chaâba's community emphasizes the way the immigrant community is subject to racism and victimization at the hands of French policy. The Chaâba remains an essentially Arab space removed from any French signs. However, this portrayal also functions to align certain characters, such as Bouzid, within a time lag, and situates their images with that of a retrograde and colonial Algeria.

Bouzid dreams of creating a virtual Algeria out of the Chaâba. He hopes to maintain the cultural traditions and community ties in France that he established in Algeria through life in the Chaâba. The camera focuses on Bouzid and his wife's daily habits, such as the morning bath and the drawing of water from the communal pump. This latter detail emphasizes the "Arabness" of the women, dressed traditionally and quarreling with one another. The opening scene focuses on Bouzid's morning routine and symbolically establishes the desire for cultural continuity with Algeria through reference to life in Algeria and the depiction of quotidian life in the Chaâba as a continuation of it. The film's second shot, viewed through the doors of the Chaâba and the gaze of its nine-year-old narrator, Omar, frames Bouzid leaving for work and receding into the distance. Viewed from the perspective of Omar, who will be situated more closely to French culture than the rest of his family, this scene quickly establishes the symbolic image of an old Algeria through the patriarchal figure of Bouzid, who recedes in the distance.[8] The film's subsequent shot continues to play on this tension between an old Algeria and the Western world, when narration begins as a voiceover by Omar, who begins to tell the story of life in the Chaâba. The effect emphasizes the proximity and cultural capital Omar has in opposition to Bouzid, whose image recedes into the distance, as Omar's voice and gaze attain control. This tension between a colonial-era Algeria and the West is further underscored by the copy of Gustave Flaubert's *Salaambô* that Omar holds, a novel that evokes Orientalist images of the colonial era and suggests the ways that Omar holds the tools to learn about the colonial victimization to which his parents could only be subject.

Reference to the narrative of nineteenth-century imperialism hovers over the representation of the Chaâba. Bouzid's dream of the Chaâba is portrayed as firmly rooted in the nineteenth century colonial conception of spatial relations, where an indigenous community, represented as filthy, loud, and barbarous, remained cloistered or sequestered from French space. We discover the Chaâba through the panoramic shots that accompany Omar and *les gones*, the "kids" in Lyonnais slang, as they run past the huts constructed of cardboard and stray materials and through the mud that serves as the décor for the community. The Chaâba is represented as a space of filth and the abject, littered with urban remains found in garbage piles. It is a space cloistered off by the Rhone on one side and the forest on the other, highlighting the eighteenth-century conception of the "savage" nature of "indigenous" community. In another direction it remains closed off to the world by a metallic gate and a major peripheral artery. It is one of only two spaces to which we have access through Ruggia's camera. The other space is that of the school and its teacher, M. Grand. Ultimately, the camera will only map these two spaces, and they remain mutually exclusive. Indeed, the camera moves outside of the Chaâba only to film the path to the school and the space of the school itself. The Chaâba, then, is defined in opposition to the French space of the school, and it is an insular and enclosed space where the signs of "indigenous" life abound, such as the women's communal washing of the laundry outside, the slaughter of sheep, and the traditional circumcision of young Omar and his friend with an accompanying celebration. In many ways, though, the establishment of these binary spatial divisions evokes the description of the "indigenous" colonial village described by Frantz Fanon, where the Arab quarter remains a place of "indigenous" life and misery clearly separated from the French colonial settler area (*Damnés* 8). The illicit nature of the Chaâba as a quasi-colonial space is underscored by the piles of garbage found on its borders. The garbage brought from the urban center to the peripheral space relegates the Chaâba to a place of colonial filth and rejection, a space only good enough to be used as a dump by the French center.

Outside of its emblematic presence in the school, France remains a phantasmatic world, unrepresented and invisible. Within the school France is represented by the "moral" lessons of M. Grand, who teaches the *beur* students about proper hygiene. The lesson is reinforced by the mud that students track from the Chaâba — traces of their dirty origin. M. Grand is frequently filmed in close-up or shot from above during such lessons, and the hexagonal map of France, at times, can be perceived in the background. The symbolism of such encounters is the greatness of racial purification, of the erasure of the colonial traces of one's origin, and of full integration into the pure map of French identity, represented by morality and the hexagonal image and structure explicated by M. Grand. Omar is a star student of such lessons, and his ability to excel is opposed to that of his rebel friend, Hacène, who, frustrated by his inabilities and by the attitudes of Grand, drives a plume pen into the hand of his teacher. Here, again, Fanon's description of the psychologically damaged and rebellious colonized who revolts against his oppressor returns to the screen in opposition to Omar's alignment with French space.[9]

While the opposition between the school and the Chaâba evokes clear colonial divisions of space and culture, other scenes within the Chaâba evoke ways of seeing and spatial arrangements informed primarily by the colonial era as well. One particular scene signals the nostalgia for an insular vision of Algerian culture tied to the colonial era. As Omar peers into a circular enclosure he views a naked bathing girl, Yasmine, named the "prisonnière du Chaâba" (Chaâba's prisoner) by his brother, Farid. We subsequently learn that Farid maintains a secretive voyeuristic relationship with her as the two boys peer in through the clapboard walls of the Chaâba that surround Yasmine. The scene appears to blatantly replicate Orientalist modes of perceiving Algerian women and evinces a harem narrative through the spatial dynamics of enclosure and secrecy. Although the theme of adolescent innocence would seemingly divest this scene of its imperialist tones, the thematics of captivity and liberation that ensue only further align the scene and its voyeuristic dynamics with the colonial era.

As families slowly leave the Chaâba for their new subsidized apartments in the HLM, Omar notes Farid's dismay that "Yasmine, la prisonnière a disparu" (Yasmine, the prisoner, has disappeared). Yasmine's move away from the Chaâba can only entail a repetition of Orientalist nostalgia, a yearning for a seemingly authentic and sexualized relationship with ties to territory conceived as insular and enclosed. Moreover, the desire for this voyeuristic relationship is mediated through a masculinist gaze that perceives the loss of the "authentic" and insular enclosure of the Chaâba as the loss of a sexualized feminine territory transformed into fantasy. This type of perception aligns the Chaâba with a colonial ideal, a space where the erotics of the Orientalist harem narrative combine with sentiments of nostalgia, desire, and territoriality. Moreover, Yasmine's liberation from the Chaâba and subsequent move into the structure of French modernity, mediated as it is by the quasi-orientalist gaze, can only take place through the thematics of enclosure and nostalgic longing for a "cultural" territory that must be lost. In the same way Omar's successful integration into the structure of French modernity functions much as does that of Yasmine; it depends upon the thematics of enclosure and retrograde evocations of an "authentic" Algeria. Such liberation can manifest itself only through a total destruction of the Chaâba, and its eventual reconstruction, in the filmic narrative, as evidenced by Omar's dream of a fire that destroys the Chaâba and his father's dream of an authentic Algerian space. While these two narratives of liberation from the Chaâba remain different, they do share the common theme of nostalgic loss and reconstruction through the autobiographical gaze of Begag mediated by Ruggia's camera. Moreover, within the filmic narrative, they both rely upon a desire to visually and spatially map territory as a familiar and retrograde vision. What is of interest, however, is the way that the characters who share this vision, Bouzid and Farid, are represented as remaining closer to an "authentic Arab" ethnicity than Omar, who must not only speak French correctly and excel in school but also envision the destruction of the only home he knows. Farid, unlike Omar, struggles at school, and he speaks in a much more heavily accented French. His integration into French society is uncertain, and his hopes for success appear linked to Omar. These traits accentuate his alignment with the Chaâba and its evocation of a colonial-era spatial aesthetics. His desire, like that of Bouzid, remains further aligned with the nostalgic gaze for a lost colonial-era topography. Both Bouzid and Farid dream of more distant ethnic realms where their vision remains enclosed in comparison to that of Omar.

The ending of the film symbolically reaffirms this distinction in visions, aligning Omar's vision with a more vertical, progressive perspective in opposition to the more horizontally aligned vision of his brother Farid, who peers into the harem and longs for such extensions of sight, and of Bouzid, who continuously envisions the map of the Chaâba as an extended, yet insular, cultural community spreading out against the horizon as an extension of Algeria. As Omar's family leaves for the HLM, the camera films the Chaâba receding into the distance (a scene similar to the recurring image of Bouzid receding into the distance). The final scene features Omar on the balcony of the family's HLM apartment, midway up the building. This vertical perspective is opposed to the more horizontal images and visions associated with Bouzid, Farid, and Yasmine in their enclosures within a more colonial-era spatial and ideological perspective.

Even given this gesture toward progressive cultural vision and integration, the film gestures toward the ways such vision might simply not suffice. Citing Maurice Carême's poem "Liberté," Omar remarks that although he will seek the stars in his new vision, "seulement, un jour je m'arretêrai" (only, one day, I will stop). Ending on this image of Omar on the HLM balcony, the film's ambiguous scene can be understood to suggest that the "beur's" path to success in France will be limited. Ending thus, it can be viewed as a quasi apologetics for assimilation and an attempt at a wider critique of social mobility in France. Viewed this way, as an attempted postcolonial intervention in recent debates about immigrants, particularly those living within the HLM, *Le Gone du Chaâba* would seemingly offer an important message. However, although the film gestures toward, or at the very least suggests, a relationship between the immediate post–Algerian War period in France and contemporary issues related to immigration, its critique of assimilation remains limited. First, the film concludes on spatial logics separating progressivism from the retrograde and the stalled. The emphasis placed on the narrator's stopping point midway up the symbolic structure of modernity and integration for France's postcolonial minorities that the HLM represents, underscores this perspective. Ultimately, the reliance upon spatial relations and mobility cast within the terms of movement and progressivism remains invested in the film's dynamics of a Western progressive sphere in opposition to its Other. The ending of the film, although suggestive of the limits imposed by Western progressivism on postcolonial minorities, gestures little to the larger construction and underlying fallacies of how and why mobility remains limited. Indeed, the very structure of spatial divisions between East and West so underscored by the film seems to lie at the heart of the problem. However, the film itself suggests a strong investment in the very distinctions that ultimately situate images of Algeria and certain

Algerian subjects in a temporally removed sphere. The film ends on a tone that suggests the victimization of the postcolonial minority figure but offers little in the way of how to overcome this type of victimization by a social structure that will ultimately not fulfill its promises. Much like the ending of *Indigènes*, the ending of *Le Gone du Chaâba* hints at a critique of the contemporary French nation and a correspondence between its return to colonial era history and contemporary forms of oppression within metropolitan France. Yet, the majority of the film, like that of *Indigènes*, establishes an investment in its characters' belonging or distance with respect to the image of the French nation. In many ways *Le Gone du Chaâba* demonstrates a fetishization of French national space; its narrative, inclusive of its ending, is driven by the very notion of movement into that space or a frustrating distancing from it.

With the exception of its ending, *Le Gone du Chaâba* represents the issue of cultural assimilation in distinct imagistic spheres: France on one side, and an Algerian community aligned more closely with the colonial era than with Western modernity on the other. Like the cartography of the Chaâba in contrast to that of the school, there is less emphasis on the blundered and blurred path in between these two spheres. Of course Omar and others from the Chaâba do negotiate between two worlds. However, the narrative of Omar's emergence requires the playing of those two worlds against one another with less emphasis on that very decision to do so and the instrumentality of those two cultural spheres.

The duality that is prevalent throughout *Le Gone du Chaâba* is without a doubt a function of the West's requirement. However, it is relevant to question whether the return to the history of immigration found in films such as *Le Gone du Chaâba* might best intervene in the question of minorities' relegation to marginal spaces through a repetition of the investment in the duality of spatial dynamics, in the portrayal of victimization as the victim's poor choice, and in the dynamics of Western progressivism versus a representation of its Other as archaic. Would a critique of Western modernity as a structure deeply rooted in colonial history work better if it were to probe the dynamics of the way the spatial distinctions that placed postcolonial minorities on the borders of France upon their arrival have evolved to keep them there today? Such a critique of the instrumentality of French nationalism would require a gesture toward the larger political and social structures of France and an engagement with contemporary narratives pertaining to that type of oppression. Of course this would entail a radically different film. Although revisionist films like *Le Gone du Chaâba* are important in the ways they raise consciousness of overlooked histories of immigration, the question remains as to whether an emphasis on colonial dynamics in a period piece might address the complexities structuring French national space and social mobility. The depiction of victimization in *Le Gone du Chaâba* remains rooted in the very cycle of victimization itself, since no real sense of how one might address its dynamics in oppositional ways is offered by the film. The film's inclusion of earlier Orientalist narratives and its depiction of the Chaâba as a virtual colonial space demonstrate the important role colonial-era narratives play in the postcolonial visual imaginary in its attempts to historicize diaspora and map victimization within metropolitan spaces. The colonial era as a central perspective remains an imperative yet problematic point of reference for *Le Gone du Chaâba* in its mapping of the victimization of postcolonial minorities in France.

In a similar manner Soraya Nini's collaboration with Philippe Faucon in the adaptation of her popular 1993 novel, *Ils disent que je suis une beurette*, also trades upon the opposition of a progressive Western perspective to a fundamentalist "Eastern" view. In her collaboration with Faucon, Nini was adamant that the film reflect the hybridity of her protagonist and of the intended title of her novel, *L'entre deux cultures*, which editorial pressures forced her to change.[10] *Samia* follows the life of a young girl of Algerian heritage growing up in the distinct spheres of French and Algerian culture. Like *Le Gone du Chaâba* the representation of this position opposes a retrograde and partial image of Algerian culture to the progressive, modernist tones of French culture. The sixth of eight children growing up in Marseille, Samia, played by Lynda Benahouda, is subject to the racist remarks of white French people as well as to the oppression of her "traditional" Muslim brother, Yacine, played by Mohamed Chaouch, who becomes a paternal figure when her father is hospitalized. Yacine forbids Samia to leave the house and subjugates her with patriarchal rhetoric. The representation of racism in France notwithstanding, the home is presented as a distinct sphere of fundamentalist oppression, where women are intended to be nothing short of subservient, and France, despite its racist remarks, is represented as a space of personal freedom and potential liberation. The depiction of Samia's liberation depends upon the alignment of Algerian culture with a distanced and remote cultural sphere.

The entire film is, in many ways, devised to play the image of a quasi-global project of liberation against that of a temporally remote and backward image of the Maghreb. *Samia*, Arabic for "the woman who stands up," is marketed globally by Pyramide Films. When it first appeared it had its own website with *court métrage*, interviews, games, and electronic cards related to the movie. Much of this marketing strategy made the film a popular success. The rebellious character of Samia, determined to not be simply a victim of the fundamentalism of Yacine and her mother, can also be understood as a component of the global reach and popularity of the film. In a review, film critic Esther Iverem, editor of SeeingBlack.com, wrote, "I vote Samia as the Black girl flick of the year . . . Samia, who swishes through the world with a thick ponytail and much attitude, could easily live in North Philly or the South Side of Chicago. She is a poster child for roll-your-neck Black girl defiance. Samia is defiant of racism in the streets and of her dysfunctional family at home. And, to top it off, she has the regular teen-ager funky surliness." Iverem is quick to identify defiance and resistance as metropolitan traits of postcolonial minorities. However, the representation of such traits in *Samia* comes about in great part through the stereotypical representation of the fundamentalist and patriarchal oppression of other Algerians living in France who are opposed to its modernity. The film depicts enforced fasting at Ramadan, traditional and ethnicized bridal and wedding showers, and a trip to the doctor to determine if the young woman's virginity is still intact.

Perhaps most telling is the representation of stereotypes about the Maghreb, such as that of the violent, patriarchal male aligned with Islamic fundamentalism. On numerous occasions Yacine rebukes Samia for her forays into French culture and for her desire to dress like a young French woman. Samia frequents a freewheeling girlfriend and flirts with a French boy. Yet, Samia's sister has run away from home from fear of reprisal by Yacine after falling in love with a French man. Like Bouzid in *Le Gone du Chaâba*, Yacine creates a quasi Chaâba of the family's living quarters within France, remarking, "Ici, c'est pas l'Amérique, à la maison tu es au bled" (This isn't America here, when you're at home, you're back home). It is interesting to note that Yacine uses America, not France, as his cultural, spatial, and temporal benchmark. The statement is also underscored by Samia's Nike backpack, emblazoned on the back with the slogan "Just Do It." Of course the slogan conjures Samia's defiance of Yacine and his traditional doctrines and aligns her more with a globalized form of modernity and progressivism. However, such oppositions ultimately align Yacine with the stereotypical image of a patriarchal, backward Arab. Moreover, his statement establishes an opposition between the Arab world and America, an opposition that, viewed within the contemporary geopolitical context, simply reflects the current polarity. Given that *Samia* ends somewhat in *media res*, we are not sure precisely where she will end. However, the ending portrays her, both literally and figuratively, standing up. She has refused the gynecological exam, and she appears to be headed for a civil career in France.

The popularity of *Samia* is due in great part to a perceived depiction of the clash of civilizations between the Muslim world and France. Most review summaries of the film, such as that of Iverem, above, and of Joshua Tanzer, noted here, are quick to point this out in noting how "it's extraordinary to see what a vast difference in expectations the parents and the children have in this island of strict Islam amid modern, cosmopolitan Marseille." Samia is clearly placed in between this perceived clash, and much like Omar in *Le Gone du Chaâba*, emerges aligned with French modernity. Her ability to overcome the abuse to which she is subject at the hands of her traditional family is without a doubt inspirational for many. However, we must recall that representations of victimization, such as that of *Samia*, are ultimately choices, choices about what type of victimization to represent and how, precisely, to represent it. The representation of victimization and its opposition in *Samia* depends upon the mapping of a certain image of the Maghreb, one that relies upon the tropes of distancing, both spatial and temporal. Ultimately, such a mapping of Algeria conjures a colonial temporality, one which finds France and Algeria cohabiting identical material spatial realms but which relegates a certain aspect of Algeria to a remote and incompatible space with respect to that of France. Films such as *Samia* are powerful precisely because there are so few of them. Their appeal is, in great part, due to their representation of the incompatibility of two civilizations that coexist within the same space.

However, what is interesting about a film like *Samia* is the way that the film never fully represents the actual "clash of civilizations," which is central to the very questions of immigration and cultural identity in France. Instead, *Samia* focuses on the polarity of West and East as a problem of temporal and spatial distinction, without addressing the underlying ways that the polarity comes to clash within the same metropolitan space. The riots in France during 2005 are a specific example of one way that the polarities of cultural identification and identity linked to political expectations clashed to signal widespread structural problems related to such spatial and temporal distinctions within the same geopolitical sphere. Moreover, the specificities of the shared colonial history between France and

Algeria that establish such clashes are never addressed in the film; this aspect of colonial history is simply elided. *Samia*'s mapping of victimization ultimately establishes a cartography that separates the stereotypes and presumptions related to France and Algeria into distant arenas without examining the specific ways they establish a cartography of violent demands and reinforced antagonism. Although the film contains no actual maps of territory, it establishes distinct spatial cartographies of France and Algeria through its representation of victimization.

Here, some comparison to Yamina Benguigui's popular first fiction film, *Inch'Allah Dimanche*, might illuminate how the representation of the transcendence of victimization, a victimization shared by both France and Algeria as part of a colonial legacy, need not be structured as a competing tension between two distinct national spheres. Exhibiting a keen interest in the colonial legacy of immigration in France, Benguigui has already produced documentary work, such as *Mémoires d'immigrées*, with classic appeal.[11] Her turn to the history of immigration in northern France in the 1970s in *Inch'Allah Dimanche* can be seen as a continuation of the narrativization of women's liberation from the victimizing tensions of cultural clash. Although the protagonist of Benguigui's film is not a *beur*, she is a character caught firmly between two different cultures, and the obstacles to liberation that she faces, although different in nature, create a situation for her that is not unlike that faced by the characters of *Samia* and *Le Gone du Chaâba*. Yet, in *Inch'Allah Dimanche*, the protagonist's victimization, although dependent upon the representation of a radically traditional and retrograde image of North African culture, ultimately serves as a path, albeit difficult, to a potentially productive union of France and Algeria within the same material space.

The film begins with the departure of its protagonist for France. Given the 1974 ruling that allows North African laborers residing in France to be reunited with their families, Zouina comes to France with her three children and evil mother-in-law, Aicha. Zouina and her husband, Ahmed, have been apart for ten years when the story begins and are essentially strangers despite Ahmed's brief visits to Algiers. Upon her arrival in France Zouina is subject not only to Aicha's constant abuse but also to the physical and psychological abuse of Ahmed, who routinely beats her and berates her according to Aicha's dictates. Not permitted to leave the house Zouina nonetheless manages to experience encounters with France and its culture, encounters that, although frequently "performative" as Mireille Rosello has argued, prove decisive for Zouina's liberation from the confines of abusive behavior and the colonial mentality evinced by Ahmed and Aicha.[12] I refer to the colonial mentality of Aicha and Ahmed here, because although both affect a traditional, quasi-fundamentalist perspective of Algerian culture and Islam, they both understand France solely as a space of opportunity, where strict cultural divisions must prevail. On the other hand, through her brief encounters with the working divorcée Mlle Briat, a neighbor who befriends her, or with a young French bus driver who passes by the family's rental house, or with a military widow whose husband was killed during the Algerian War, Zouina strives toward a certain meeting place between worlds, which does not exclude them and which will, potentially, establish a space outside the abusive rhetoric and practice of traditionalism gone awry.

In many ways Zouina's victimization is represented as being a result of an impossible meeting point of any substance between Algeria and France, since Aicha and Ahmed are ultimately afraid of encounters between the two cultures, and this engenders their abuse. The key, then, for Zouina remains the "contact zone" between cultures, which enables her to act as an agent of change and transformation within her abusive family.[13] Ultimately, this movement between cultures and colonial spatial logics, transported within the postcolonial metropolis, establishes a collective form of memory that maps Algeria and France as complex yet united cultural spheres.

One of the most salient examples of encounter that transcends the colonial logic of victimization can be seen in Zouina's encounter with Mathilde, the widow of a French military officer killed in the Algerian War. Zouina first encounters Mathilde on one of her clandestine Sunday outings with her children. While Ahmed and Aicha are away, Zouina escapes from the house with her children to explore. Zouina encounters Mathilde by chance in a cemetery where military veterans are buried. The cemetery conjures the haunting and shared memories of colonial warfare, and we soon learn that Mathilde is still mourning the loss of her husband in Algeria. Zouina's relationship with Mathilde evolves to the point where images of Algeria are presented to her through Mathilde. Zouina first encounters the images of the Algerian landscape through the photos that adorn the walls of Mathilde's home. Later, Mathilde offers Zouina a picture book of Algeria, which will ultimately be destroyed because of Aicha's rage and alignment with an insular colonial-type mentality. Further, Mathilde will try to help Zouina locate another Algerian family living in town. In all of these instances the film focuses on potential meeting points between Algeria and France, between land, culture, and historical lineages. As Rosello points out, such encounters demonstrate that these characters "have not accepted the supposedly final and definitive fracture between France and Algeria, between the French and the Algerian people. All these characters acknowledge the consequences of a bloody war of liberation between an ex-colonial power and its colonized land and still refuse to sever historical and cultural links between the two lands" (*France* 22). I would add that what enables encounters such as that between Mathilde and Zouina is also the refusal of the victim's position in relationship to colonial history and its structuring of cultural relations. Refusal of the victim's position in relationship to patriarchal colonial history, for both Zouina and Mathilde, enables a meeting point. The fact that the initial encounter between these two women takes place within the cemetery suggests a transcendence of traditional spaces of interdiction established by history. Zouina escapes the confines of the home as dictated by Ahmed, and Mathilde transcends the confines of historical antagonism represented by the Algerian War, which the cemetery evokes.

Both women gesture toward such encounters outside the paradigm of historical victimization through a continued relationship.

Moreover, the film underscores the imperative of seeing beyond the paradigm of victimization through its depiction of Malika Bouira, the mother of the Algerian family that Zouina wants so desperately to meet. Much to Zouina's chagrin, however, Malika proves to be victim to her husband and to the dictates of traditionalism. She is relegated to the house and to her husband's orders. As Malika realizes that Zouina is more aligned with the French world outside the home, she throws Zouina out of her house. The scene ends with Malika beating her chest in distress behind the closed door of the house as Zouina desperately attempts to make a connection with her from the outside. Here, as elsewhere, victimization to the mentality of enclosed, insular spheres separating France from Algeria is the underlying reason for a history of further victimization.

Zouina's return home after her visit with Malika proves decisive. Upon her return, with Aicha and the neighbors looking on, Zouina stands her ground with Ahmed, explaining that from then on she will take the children to school. Aicha cries that the French are to blame, and Ahmed tells her to retreat to the house, seemingly accepting Zouina's stance. Here, the film suggests that the insular nature of cultural spheres dividing French and Algerians is a retrograde notion.

Although no easy route to emancipation is offered to the spectator at the end of *Inch'Allah Dimanche*, the film's close implies that it is through the refusal to accept the impossible cultural encounter dividing French and Algerian spaces and cultures, espoused by Aicha and Malika for example, that the cycle of victimization might be broken. Of course the refusal of victimization is what ultimately enables the facilitating encounter in the first place. In Benguigui's film the refusal of victimization takes place through its transformation from within the family unit. Zouina is able to effect change from within the confines of abusive behavior. The clash of civilizations is revealed to be more of a function of the actual separation and lack of cultural dialogue between cultures than of anything else. While Samia is able to transcend victimization through the creation of a retrograde image of Algerian culture, Zouina is able to do so through a mediating perspective that enables, at the very least, a potentially wider meeting point for different cultural perspectives.

Merzak Allouache's film *L'Autre monde* was inspired by the filmmaker's desire to represent the clash of civilizations in Algeria through the experiences of two *beur* lovers, Yasmine and Rachid. Like *Samia*, the film was conceived as a representation of the experiences of the *beur* woman and her liberation and designed to have wider implications for the condition of Algerian women. As Allouache states in a letter outlining his intentions in the filmmaking process: "L'héroïne de 'l'Autre monde' est une femme, française et d'origine algérienne. A travers elle, ainsi que d'autres femmes qu'elle rencontre au cours de son voyage, je veux rendre hommage aux femmes algériennes dont le courage n'a eu aucune limite durant ces années de plomb" (The heroine of *L'Autre monde* is a French woman of Algerian origin. Through her, as well as through the women she encounters during her voyage, I wanted to render homage to the Algerian women whose courage has had no limit during these leaden years).[14] However, unlike *Le Gone du Chaâba* and *Samia*, *L'Autre monde* situates the action and the focus of representation in Algeria, rather than France. Moreover, the film attempts to engage with contemporary postcolonial problems in Algeria directly, and, in many ways, it does just this through its engagement with the confusing and uncertain political landscape of Islamic fundamentalism and civil warfare. Throughout his career Allouache has been concerned with tackling the complexities of Algeria in the period of decolonization. His feature film *Omar Gatlato* (1976) was set in the neighborhood of Bab el-Oued in Algiers and was heralded such a success for its treatment of the place of fundamentalism in relationship to Western values that it revolutionized the course of Algerian cinema. The Algerian public had a taste for complex films treating contemporary realities in Algeria. Allouache distinguished himself in 1989 when he made the documentary *L'après-*

octobre (Following October) about the Paris riots of 1988 that took place in the suburbs. *L'après-octobre*, like *L'Autre monde*, sought to inscribe a wider conception of the clash of civilizations that had divided the image of Francophone society into a Western sphere and an Arab sphere. However, although *L'Autre monde* does indeed engage with such images of the clash of civilizational values that pit fundamentalism against Western influence in Algeria, it ultimately situates the images of this "new Algeria" within a certain Western perspective of an unchanging, violent, and repetitive landscape.

The film begins when Yasmine awakens one morning to discover that Rachid, bothered by reports of contemporary violence and civil warfare in Algeria, has left Paris for Algeria only to be conscripted in the Algerian army. Rachid's departure is due to an identity crisis of sorts that remains nebulous within the film. Yasmine, who has never been to Algeria and speaks only French, feels compelled to search for him when he disappears. We learn later that his troop was ambushed by terrorists and he is listed as missing. In many ways the film rehearses the popular theme of a woman who refuses to give up her man to the vagaries of history and calls to mind films such as Flora Gomes's *Mortu Nega* and Sarah Maldoror's *Sambizanga*.[15]

Yasmine's trip to Algeria becomes a confusing attempt to decipher a landscape she has only encountered through the stories of her immigrant parents in Paris. At the outset of the film, with Western classical choral music playing, we see Yasmine shopping for a *djellabah* and *hidjab* that she wears back to her apartment. The implication is that Yasmine believes she will need to wear them throughout her trip. However, upon her arrival in Algiers, she encounters her Westernized uncle and cousin, who tell her to remove the veil. Much of the representation of Algiers conforms to that of the Western world, and the otherness in the film's title is not readily apparent. However, the setting of 1999 in Algeria is one of terror, and this context frames Yasmine's exploration and apprenticeship of her country of heritage. When she inquires about the terror, Yasmine's cousin informs her that the whole country has slipped into a form of amnesia. However, when Yasmine avows that she will search the provinces for Rachid, her cousin warns her of the dangerous terrorists roaming the hills. Indeed, distinct spheres opposing a Westernized world to a dangerous "Other" world emerge at this point and function to structure the remainder of the film. En route to the rural scene where Rachid presumably disappeared, Yasmine is taken prisoner by a band of young, armed fundamentalists led by their "Emir." The group, we learn, is caught in a self-perpetuating cycle of terror, murder, and abuse without any grounding ideology. With the help of Hakim, a terrorist who betrays his comrades to help her, Yasmine is able to escape. The depiction of the fundamentalist Hakim seeks to provide a certain glimpse into his humanity. Tenacious, Yasmine is able to persevere and eventually ends up living in a whorehouse on the edge of the Algerian desert, where an apocalyptic ending arrives on the day of the new millennium to destroy all and symbolically make way for a new Algerian political and social topography.

In making *L'Autre monde* Allouache claimed that his inspiration to film in Algeria derived from a strong desire to "sortir des images de ce pays" (get outside the images of this country), and from his frustration with "un pays en guerre dont les images s'estompaient au fil du temps jusqu'à ne plus être que des flashs rapides et routiniers du journal télévisé" (a country at war, the images of which amount to nothing more than the quick and routine flashes of the six o'clock news). Ironically, however, in *L'Autre monde*, Rachid and Yasmine return to the "old country" only to become a flash of the new violence themselves. They participate in a repetitive colonial-era history of violence.

Allouache's desire to reveal an authentic, Algerian landscape in *L'Autre monde* through his wish to get outside the images of violence in Algeria, and his desire to unveil the real complexities of Algeria to Yasmine, echo Benjamin Stora's frustration with visual representations of Algeria in the '90s. In his study of the visual imaginary and contemporary representations of Algeria, *La guerre invisible: Algérie, années 90*, Stora argues that a pervasive focus on colonial history precludes a representation of contemporary civil warfare in Algeria: "cette absence d'Algérie est forcément gênante. Eclipse des paysages, défection de langue, omission des acteurs de la guerre (militaries ou islamistes), tout ce qui est directement vécu ne parvient pas à se retrouver dans la representation visuelle" (this absence of Algeria is necessarily troubling. Eclipse of scenery, defection from language, omission of the actors of war [military or Islamist], all that is directly lived cannot be found in visual representation) (92). Stora's analysis of the visual dynamics of representations of contemporary Algeria perceptively acknowledges the fixity of the colonial period in the postcolonial cultural imaginary as a haunting presence: "Reste que le conflit actuel ne peut décidément être perçu qu'à travers le prisme ancien de la période coloniale française" (It remains that the current conflict can only be perceived through the old prism of the French colonial period) (88). Stora very perceptively suggests that current civil warfare in Algeria remains linked to a retrospective interpretation of history unable to surpass colonial victimization. Further, he notes the essential opaque and unrepresentable nature of contemporary Algeria: "Trois ans après le début du conflit, le sentiment existe déjà d'une impossible visibilité de cette guerre, du voile opaque qui l'entoure, de la nécessité de le déchirer" (Three years following the beginning of this conflict, the sentiment of an impossible visibility surrounding this war, of a veil that shrouds it, and of the necessity of tearing it open still exists) (73).[16] Although Stora's language might seemingly suggest a haunting, neo-orientalist desire to "tear open the veil," or to observe it being torn open, it is important to note that his discourse does not iterate a retrograde vision of Algeria through such statements but seeks to reveal the contemporary nature of Algeria from the perspective of the present. Stora's desire to tear open the veil can be likened to disposing of the shroud of colonial-era images and aura attached to it as cultural signifier.

In many ways Allouache sets out to do the same in *L'Autre monde*. However, the veil cast away, both in reality and symbolically, colonial-era victimization returns to the screen to subsume Yacine and

Rachid within it. Although Allouache hopes to reveal a new landscape to the Western perspective of Yasmine, and consequently to the Western viewer, his film ultimately replicates colonial-era tropes. Yasmine, threatened and imprisoned as she is by masculine violence, becomes part of the postmodern flash of violence. This apocalyptic tone imprisons her within a fragmented, yet static and timeless, geocultural Algerian space.[17] In many ways we might say that she is liberated to see a new Algerian landscape only to find her way into a postmodern version of a colonial-era captivity narrative, where the woman's body remains trapped and threatened within a "timeless" Eastern enclosure. The "other world" that Yasmine discovers and experiences proves to be less marked by alterity than by the same old images of colonial violence and victimization.

Allouache's film is an important and experimental attempt to move beyond the colonial-era images of Algeria that populate cinema and popular culture, particularly in France. His work offers, in many ways, a glimpse into an Algeria that is not often filmed. Yet, the cartographic experience that Yasmine, who is born in France, has in her roaming through Algerian landscapes and culture ultimately transforms itself into a mapping out of Algeria that is closely linked to the repetitive narrative of colonial victimization. Although Allouache's film is fictional, and less inspired by autobiographical experiences like *Le Gone du Chaâba* and *Samia*, it is nonetheless driven by socio-realist dynamics. The representation of the cyclical violence and victimization seen through a character living between "worlds" is certainly in line with what we know to be a reality in contemporary Algeria. Much the same could be said of certain portrayals of the situation of immigrants and their children discussed in *Le Gone du Chaâba* and *Samia*. However, when colonial era tropes, accurate as they may be within the scope of the realities of contemporary Algeria and its diaspora, function as elements that visually propel filmic narratives, we must ask how the very critique of that type of victimization might ever emerge as an oppositional narrative.

Do films such as those discussed in this chapter ultimately participate in the Algeria Syndrome, characterized by the obsessive centrality of France's Algerian histories?[18] To the extent that these films all turn backward in a socio-realist mode to address the question of Algeria as a colonial specter, we would have to concede that they all constitute a part of that syndrome in different ways. However, a clear distinction can be seen to prevail in the way that the question of Algeria and its legacy are represented. Benguigui's *Inch'Allah Dimanche*, with its gesture toward a transcendence of the colonial divisions of the Algerian War, would seem to point in a direction that would like to map a new history outside the colonial paradigm. The ability to envision and embrace this history from beyond the victim's perspective, as the comparison established in this chapter suggests, will ultimately determine to what degree the lingering maladies of colonial history continue to dominate our vision.

5

Colonial Cinema and the Aesthetics of Postcolonial Victimization

Pépé le Moko and Assia Djebar's *La Disparition de la langue française*

In this chapter I would like to adopt a perspective that will supplement the focus on the visual nature of postcolonial victimization discussed in the preceding chapters. I have attempted to show that in postcolonial francophone cinema on North Africa, the visualization of territory to be reclaimed from the colonial past remains central to revisionist history. Frequently, the centrality of territory and the contestation over it common to the age of terror engender narratives of victimization, narratives that ultimately establish competing images of martyrdom, victims, and territorial propriety. Often, these narratives remain focused on the victimization that took place during the colonial era and, even when founded by the best intentions, often overlook the relationship between colonial history and contemporary forms of oppression and victimization. The cartographic process of creating maps of victimization is, in many ways, homologous to the creation of discursive narratives of victimization. Not only is the process which maps the spaces and subjects of victimization an act that generates narratives, in the largest sense of the term, it is also a gesture firmly rooted in a larger discursive network of victimization that ultimately influences it. The mapping of victimization takes place as a response to the historical narrative of victimization, and it is often grounded in an attempt to view and make others see the sites and subjects of victimization differently or as integral and whole after the debilitating effects of colonial terror and oppression. In this chapter I examine the interplay of colonial history and the contemporary age of terror that occurs in the attempt to create written narrative from a colonial-era text adapted into a film. This chapter, then, is as much about the attempt to map a colonial-era film, its sites and themes, within a postcolonial novel, as it is about the way that the adaptation of that colonial-era narrative is already mapped out by larger narratives of victimization.

Assia Djebar's novel *La Disparition de la langue française* is an exercise in the theoretical problem of the generation of narratives of victimization and their relationship to seeing outside the paradigm established by colonial history. Djebar's text is, in many ways, an experiment in whether a return to the visual sites of colonial history in North Africa can function as a starting point, or point of historical return, from which to envision or map the experience of the formerly colonized nation differently. Djebar's novel functions as a rewriting or narrativization of Julien Duvivier's classic colonial-era film *Pépé le Moko* (1937). Duvivier's film was itself an adaptation of Henri La Barthe's novel of the same name. Djebar's return to Duvivier's film in *La Disparition de la langue française* can be viewed as an exposition of the very problem of establishing narratives that would envision the formerly colonized nation from a perspective not haunted or vexed by the cyclical vision of colonial victimization. The novel examines what happens when colonial aesthetics (sites, monuments, and images) and their recall of colonial oppression serve as points of departure for new narratives and potentially renewed postcolonial vision. While the focus of this chapter is not on actual cinematic portrayals of the colonial period, Djebar's examination of the way that spectatorship and viewing interact with the memory of colonial victimization within the context of contemporary terror in Algeria does inform the larger relationship between cinema and narratives of victimization. Moreover, Djebar is not only an award-winning novelist but also a filmmaker deeply interested in probing the representational limits of terrorism. In this respect, viewing and the creation of postcolonial narratives of victimization in Djebar's novel *La Disparition de la langue française* are cast against the backdrop of contemporary Algeria and its current civil warfare.

Djebar's critique of victimization proceeds carefully in the novel, demonstrating how interest in colonial victimization can easily replicate the victim's posture, exacerbate the cult of victimization in the postcolony and elsewhere, and ultimately play into the hands of those victimizers (for example, fundamentalist terrorists) who act in the name of victimization. Djebar's novel ultimately repudiates the fascination with or concentration on colonial victimization in the postcolonial world and demonstrates how such an ideological position ultimately only creates more victims, one history of violence replicating another as a spectral apparition.

The novel is set in 1991, a year that saw the beginnings of a civil war led by Islamic fundamentalists after the rejection of the results of elections won by the FIS (Islamic Salvation Front). Vexed by that move, the party began to excise its loss through its own reign of terror. Since that time extremist ideology with its monolinguism, Arabization campaign, and singular notions of cultural identity has held Algeria in its bloody grip, what Benjamin Stora has referred to as a repetition of the Algerian War, "ce besoin de répétition d'une guerre à l'autre" (this need for repetition from one war to the other) (*La guerre* 65).[1] Stora refers to the colonial war fought between 1954 and 1961 here because the contemporary conflict in Algeria has in many ways reincarnated its dynamics. The notion of a singular identity opposed to Western culture is very similar to ideology employed during the colonial war. Yet, Djebar is careful to demonstrate that this contemporary form of Algerian nationalism is nonetheless different in the way it has ruthlessly appropriated and imposed a singular cultural identity within a liberated territory, essentially replicating the underpinnings of colonization.[2] Throughout her work Djebar laments the repression and, indeed, death of pluralism imposed by this ideology and ultimately sustained by a state politics: "Ils ont sali le mot peuple, ils ont usé à tort et à travers du vocable de nation; ils ont soliloqué avec le mot Algérie, comme si cette réalité-là n'avait pas eu de multiples yeux, pour les regarder dans leur pitoyable comédie, comme si elle n'avait pas gardé ses souterraines voix pour les en assourdir!" (They have dirtied the expression "people," they have sallied in every way possible the idea of nation; they have appropriated for their sole purpose the word Algeria, as if that reality didn't have multiple eyes with which to observe their pitiful comedy, as if it hadn't kept its subterranean voices in order to render them voiceless) (*Voix* 22). Throughout Djebar's work the denouncement of radical nationalism in Algeria is part of a larger commentary on all forms of extremist ideology that seek to appropriate territory through violent ideology.[3] Written with this contextual backdrop *La Disparition de la langue française* represents a commentary on the imperative of seeing and filming narratives outside the paradigm of colonial victimization, which frequently aligns with narratives of contemporary terror.

What is central to the alignment of cinema and narratives of victimization for Djebar, then, is the age-old question of how to represent colonial history and its victimization without entering into the divisive contest over cultural and ideological territory. Yet, what Djebar demonstrates in her return to colonial history and its aesthetics in *La Disparition de la langue française* is the way that spectatorship and social narratives of victimization align with one another in important and often tragic ways.

Even the visual aesthetic that, according to Djebar, would provide the potential for creation or renewed forms of the representation of social space confronts the author with a haunting violence: "Oui, passer à la création audiovisuelle . . . pour me confronter, pour me mesurer et donc produire, c'est-à-dire inventer (et l'on n'invente, disait récemment Jacques Derrida à Lisbonne, que l'impossible) — inventer, oui, le face-à-face avec quoi, sinon avec la violence crue, avec le mal hurlant et délirant, avec le meurtre et la pas omniprésent de la mort, là-bas, chez moi" (Yes, to shift to audiovisual creation . . . to confront myself, to measure myself and therefore, to produce, that is, to invent [and one only invents, said Jacques Derrida recently in Lisbon, the impossible] — to invent, yes, the confrontation with what, if not with raw violence, with howling, delirious evil, with murder and the omnipresent footfall of death, there, back home) (*Voix* 172). Inevitably, this space of invention, of the impossible, from where the visual and the discursive emerge is marked by a foundational violence or trauma, a space — to slightly modify Michael Taussig's expression — of extreme death.[4] The question of narrating in images becomes a truly formalistic one since the disaster represents a part of the reality of contemporary Algeria but must be dislodged from its privileged occupation of social space: "Mais d'une façon ou d'une autre, resurgiraient, sans doute en arrière-plan, quels paysages d'aujourd'hui de la désolation, de la destruction? . . . Comment se placer dès lors, comment cadrer, quoi évoquer de biais dirais-je, en m'approchant peu à peu, en reculant quand il y a excès (j'appelle ici 'excès' le défaut de sur-nommer car la face de la haine, filmée trop à plat, ne signifie plus rien, se banalise alors qu'il faut laisser sourdre quel mystère, quelle horreur?)" (But one way or another, doubtless in the background, which landscapes of today's desolation and destruction would rise again? . . . How to locate oneself from then on, how to center, what to evoke sideways, I'd say, approaching slowly, backing away when there is excess [by "excess" here, I mean the mistake of over naming because the face of hate, filmed too directly no longer signifies anything, becomes banal when one must allow what mystery, what horror to seep out?]) (*Voix* 174). Contemporary social conditions are equated to a guilty and incestuous foundational myth: "Quoi montrer, quoi mettre en jeu, quoi jouer et revivre, devant l'oeil terne et vorace de la mort. Œil crevé" (What to show, what to bring into play, what to play and relive before the dull and voracious eye of death. Gauged eye) (*Voix* 174). The blind oedipal eye of the Algerian nation is not an uncommon theme in *Ces voix qui m'assiègent*. Djebar writes of the inability of Algeria to see its way through the tunnel of darkness, which is nothing more than the images of a colonial past that haunt with the reflections of an occidental presence, impelling an interdiction of diversity, "le multiple," and driving toward an oedipal and incestuous blindness. Djebar's most famous predecessors in the refutation of the oedipal figure as a form of anticolonial discourse were without a doubt Gilles Deleuze and Félix Guattari in their seminal work *Anti-Oedipus*: "Oedipus is always colonization pursued by other means; it is the interior colony" (200). Much like Deleuze and Guattari, Djebar uses the oedipal figure and its motifs of guilt, criminality, singularity, and blindness as a means of demonstrating how the violence of French colonization has become interiorized within the Algerian nation as another form of imperialism exercised by Algerian nationals.

Throughout *Ces voix qui m'assiègent*, as well as elsewhere in her work, Djebar repeats the theme of a masculine oedipal blindness and incestuous violence to underscore the tradition of obscuring Algerian plurality. Writing of the imposed monolinguism plaguing Algeria, Djebar evokes the symbol of empty, defective eyes: "Alors le meurtre surgit, le sang gicle, le refus de l'entre-deux des paroles et des langues en mouvement fait plonger dans un antre obscur. La goule — c'est-à-dire la mort vorace — rejoue son rôle funèbre. Un tel pays, dès lors, se plombe et s'obscurcit — pays soudain muet et aux yeux vides" (So murder surges, blood spurts, the refusal of plurality, of words and languages in motion causes a plunge into a dark lair. The ghoul — that is, voracious death — replays his funereal role. Such a country, from then on, becomes leaden and dark — a country suddenly mute with empty eyes) (33). This *antre* (lair) homophonic play on *entre* (between), or the conduit between languages and cultures that would foster plurality, becomes a defective space of death, where singular, violent relations inhere: "un antre — en anglais a cave — c'est-à-dire un ventre noir, une cave obscure, comment s'enfentera peu à peu un écrit pour les créateurs?" (a lair — in English a cave — that is, a dark belly, a dark cave, how to give birth little by little to a writing for creators?) (33). Djebar questions, while employing two languages of the West in translation, how an Algerian feminine, obscured by a singular violent drive, might ever create. The oedipal nature of relations impedes creation and an incipient productivity in Algeria with a blinding force.

For Djebar the visual realm is directly related to the collective experience of the nation, to the reflection of how a nation sees itself and its past. The challenge for Djebar thus comes in viewing and filming a nation that, in many ways, is just coming to sight after the long experience of being told by a colonial presence how to see itself, and at the same time demonstrating how that nation refuses to see itself now, to reflect upon its own blindness and civil warfare. In this case Algeria's failed transition to functional independence in the wake of colonial rule is integral.

Benjamin Stora has suggested that aesthetic representations within Algeria have demonstrated a haunting of the nation by its colonial history, a representational pattern that demonstrates the inability of the Algerian nation to represent and to see itself outside of the paradigm of colonial history. According to Stora, fiction, both cinematic and literary, remains haunted by "un caractère mémoriel détaché de toute représentation réaliste" (a memorial character detached from all realist representation) (*La guerre* 86). The current civil conflict in Algeria is thus eclipsed by its representation as a replay of the colonial war: "Reste que le conflit actuel ne peut décidément être perçu qu'à travers le prisme ancien de la période coloniale française" (It stands that the current conflict can only be perceived through the old prism of the French colonial period) (*La guerre* 88). Stora very perceptively suggests that current civil warfare in Algeria remains linked to a retrospective interpretation of history unable to surpass colonial victimization. Djebar's conceptualization of the visual domain remains committed to countering this tendency and to engaging with the nation and its subjects from a contemporary perspective that, without neglecting colonial history, takes into account Algeria's complex national history.

La Disparition de la langue française is about the return of the colonial era in many ways. The novel centers on the return of its Algerian protagonist, Berkane, to Algeria after his long-term residence in France. The text stages a critique of the memorial process by which the aestheticization of colonial-era victimization becomes conflated with state politics. Berkane launches into a critique of the way the Algerian government uses the memory of colonial victimization to fuel a regime of fundamentalist terror that opposes the Algerian nation as perpetual victim to an oppressive West: "Quant au souvenir de la "bataille d'Alger," on s'est contenté de remplacer les noms souvent évocateurs du passé colonial par simplement les noms d'état civil de tant de victimes de la répression de 57! N'est-ce pas le lot de cette anesthésie des mémoires en pays du tiers-monde? Comme si l'inscription des souffrances sur les lieux eux-mêmes n'existait pas plus qu'un tampon: le nom! Un point, c'est tout! N'est-ce pas là la preuve que la société entière, à bout de souffle, court en avant, se précipite en aveugle vers les tâches de survie élémentaire?" (As for the memory or the "Battle of Algiers," they settled for simply replacing the often evocative names of the colonial past with the names of so many victims of the repression of '57! Isn't that what this anesthesia of the memories of third world countries amounts to? As if the inscription of the suffering in these places was nothing more than a rubber stamp: the name! Period! Doesn't that prove that all of society, breathless, runs ahead, blindly rushing toward the task of simple survival?) (88). Far from being a rejection of the memory of the colonial period, this passage constitutes a critique of the process by which the victim's identity is appropriated by the state in order to create a colonial "memory site," a memory site closely tied to the politics of national identity in Algeria. This critique takes aim at the way the complexity of colonial history is simplified in the creation of monuments commemorating the nation's status as victim of colonial history.[5] Djebar's attention to the way that the visual inscription of colonial victimization circulates and shapes the collective national vision in this passage is critical to her exposition of the problem of mapping the spaces of colonial victimization within the context of fundamentalist terror ravaging Algeria. Her use of Duvivier's film, its themes of imprisonment and exile and their aesthetics from the colonial era, is central to the question her text poses of whether it is possible to return to colonial-era victimization without simply fulfilling its vicious cycle in the transcription of the aesthetics of the colonial era into postcolonial narrative. In many ways this experience in seeing beyond colonial history in such a way that it might inform the age of terror becomes filtered through Berkane's return to the sites of colonial Algeria that he experienced as a child.

Djebar's reexamination of the memory of colonialism and its aesthetics rests largely on the diverse references that emanate from the representation of the Casbah, the neighborhood in which Berkane spent his childhood. Although it represents the mythic place of the quest, and thus, by convention, of freedom, the Casbah and its labyrinthine structure also represent imprisonment in the spatial structure of colonialism. Here, Djebar's text recalls the cartographic process, witnessed in *Pépé le Moko*, of marking space as a dichotomous structure where liberty and imprisonment coexist.[6] Within the police headquarters, Duvivier's camera signals the Casbah on a map of Algiers as a prison house where Pépé and his "ilk" find freedom. With the police discussing how they might pursue Pépé within the Casbah, his criminal record as a thief having led them to him in Algeria, a dolly shot toward a map of Algiers represents the Casbah clearly marked in its center. The shot is followed by a dissolve to the city and the Arab quarter and then followed by another dissolve back to the police headquarters. While the cinematographic language of the shots depicts the Casbah as an impenetrable space for the police and, consequently, a place of freedom for Pépé, it also suggests that the Casbah remains a space of consequence and eventual imprisonment, since the police ultimately await the moment Pépé steps out of the Casbah.[7] Situating the center of the novel within the Casbah and the memories of colonialism it incarnates for Berkane therein, Djebar reinscribes the Casbah in the same vein as Duvivier's aesthetic; it becomes a site of ephemeral liberation that will ultimately lead the protagonist to his tragic end. Like Pépé, Berkane's liberation by the images reflected in the space of the Casbah, which reside outside it in the temporal plane of the past and impossible future, ultimately only establishes the illusion of escape that will lead to his tragic end. In this sense we must remember that Duvivier's film ends on Pépé's ineluctable destiny. Standing at the gates of the dock, Pépé peers at Gaby's departing ship, a ship returning to Paris. Faced with perpetual imprisonment within the Casbah or impending capture by the police, he draws a knife from his jacket and stabs himself. For Pépé, as for Berkane, the Casbah remains a place where the fullness of the present cannot be lived outside the parameters of tragedy.

Djebar's text plays on the return to the memory of colonialism and the formal and thematic qualities of Duvivier's film to cast Berkane's existential drama as an issue of national collective fate within the larger context of fundamentalist terror. Her remapping of Duvivier's film within the novel explores the contours of victimization as a return to the aesthetics of colonial-era history in multiple ways: it seeks to remap the spatial victimization to which Pépé is subject within the postcolonial context of Algeria (by this I mean Pépé's imprisonment within the labyrinthine Casbah), and it seeks to reinscribe Duvivier's colonial-era film itself, and its aesthetics of victimization, within the context of the postcolonial terror ravaging Algeria. The novel and the Casbah thus become an experiment in the generation of a postcolonial narrative based upon colonial aesthetics and victimization that might reveal a different trajectory. Moreover, the use of Duvivier's film within the postcolonial Algerian context suggests an attempt to transgress the reflected images of Western criminal history within the Algerian context. Given the film's emphasis on French theft and crime and their reflection within the Casbah, the site of colonial insurrection and indigenous settlement, Djebar's intertextual reference to *Pépé le Moko* is also a commentary on the possibility of seeing beyond the image and legacy of the theft that is colonialism, beyond victimization. That image of theft is reflected in the narrative of fundamentalist nationalism in Algeria and becomes, as Djebar's novel will show, an organizing principle of the way the Algerian subject experiences the present.

Djebar filters this experiment through that of Berkane and his experience and visual perception of the Casbah. Having just returned to the Casbah of his childhood and adolescence, Berkane notes, "Ainsi s'envole mon imagination vers les rues de cette Casbah, juste avant les 'événements' comme disaient les Français [. . .] je vis, je revis chez nous!" (Thus my imagination gravitates to the streets of this Casbah, just before the "events" as the French used to say [. . .] I'm living, I'm living again at home!) (14–15). "Living again" here suggests the spectral and visual quality of a ghost, and signifies at once a rebirth and a repetition of the past. It is here, between these two terms, that the Casbah will become a place located simultaneously "here" and elsewhere. Mythical site of colonial insurrections, the Casbah represents the spatial structure of the past where images of colonial victimization will reappear everywhere to haunt Berkane, and to make of him a victim of colonial aesthetics.[8]

This process is marked by nostalgia for the past. In photographing places in the Casbah, Berkane hopes to create a series of photos "de plus en plus délavée" (more and more faded) (37). The faded aspect of these photos leads to the dream of flight. Imagining his daydreaming before the proof of a faded and enlarged photo of the cupola of a mosque, Berkane notes: "Je me plongerais dans cette vision; je finirais par m'endormir: dans l'illusion de m'évader, je croirais m'en aller" (I will dive into this vision; I'll end up falling asleep: in the illusion of escaping, I'll believe I'm leaving) (37). The problem presented here is that the protagonist has only just returned to the Casbah of his birth. Here, the present can only be experienced through a vision of the place located neither in the present nor in the contemporary Casbah, but elsewhere. The aesthetic that would inscribe a faded and distant past prevents the subject from living in the Casbah in the present.[9] Moreover, it is significant that the illusion of escape be incited by the image of the mosque. The implication, as we will discover later in the novel, is that Islamic fundamentalism is predicated on the illusions of liberty and escape through the anesthetizing images of colonial-era victimization. Berkane's later disappearance at the hands of fundamentalists confirms the implication here that Islamic extremism is related to a certain way of seeing the colonial era and its images.

Berkane's nostalgic vision conditions his interpretation of everything he views, transforming objects and places into colonial mementos of victimization. Standing in the square in front of *La Pêcherie*, for instance, Berkane's thoughts turn to the invasion of Charles X and the French Army: "Cette plongée en arrière me saisit chaque fois que je reviens sur cette place, comme si c'était moi qui reculais dans la mécanique du Temps en l'occurrence, plus d'un siècle et demi. Pourquoi cette vision obsédante?" (This fall backward seizes me every time that I come back to this square, as if it were I going back into the mechanics of Time, in this case, more than a century and a half ago. Why this obsessive vision?) (78). Answering his rhetorical question, Berkane remarks that "ce qui anime mon regard rétroactif" (what animates my retroactive gaze) is an archealogy of loss, a history of imperialist disaster: "une dévastation sous nos pieds, un cimetière de mosquées, de palais, de maisons . . . tout cela abattu en trois, quatre ou cinq ans, après juillet 1830" (devastation under us, a cemetery of mosques, of palaces, of abodes . . . all this taken down in three, four or five years, after July 1830) (78). Berkane's nostalgia for the past is linked to the images of victimization that emerge from the vestiges of colonial aesthetics adorning the square, "cette place d'armes à la française" (this French military square) (79). What consumes Berkane and distances him from the present is the fascinating imagery of colonial destruction and loss: "La destruction, dis-je, tu sais combien c'est pour moi une douloureuse fascination"

(Destruction, I say, you know how much of a melancholic fascination it is for me) (78). Fascinated by colonial memory sites of loss, Berkane's vision is profoundly anchored in the temporality of colonial history, unable to register the present fully.

This inability to engage with the landscapes of Algeria from the perspective of the present is further confirmed by the way Berkane sees the territory and people he encounters. Writing to Marise, the lover he left behind in Paris, Berkane notes that the photographs he has taken of his excursions outside and around the village of Douaouda should be best understood "par référence à Eugène Fromentin" (through reference to Eugène Fromentin), the French colonial-era painter and writer whose fascination with the Algerian landscape produced numerous visual and written portrayals.[10] Berkane remarks that his photos could be entitled, following Fromentin's work, "mon automne au Sahel" (my autumn in Sahel) (83). Here, as elsewhere, Berkane's return to the landscapes of the past can only be viewed and interpreted through the colonial optic.

This vision is steeped in a desire to see the present from the colonialist perspective, or at the very least through the colonial optic characterized by a feminized quality, a viewpoint evident in his discussion of the veiled women he encounters on the streets of the Casbah: "Passantes au voile blanc de soie et de satin . . . Vont-elles se présenter à lui, les invisibles trop visibles à cause de ce regard insistant" (Passersby in the white veil of satin and silk . . . Will they show themselves to him, these too visible invisible women rendered such by the insistent gaze) (69). Berkane's desire to see the "unveiled" Algerian woman is linked to the colonialist desire described by Frantz Fanon to penetrate a "real" or authentic Algerian landscape, feminized by the male gaze. For Fanon the unveiling of the Algerian woman is aligned with rape and the violent appropriation of colonialism: "In a European's dream, the rape of the Algerian woman is always preceded by the tearing of the veil" (*Dying* 25). Fanon analyzed the visual perception of an Algerian feminine according to two temporalities: a time before the Algerian Revolution during which colonialism was "settled in a perspective of eternity," and the period of the Algerian Revolution during which unveiling served as a strategic maneuver on the part of Algerians who alternately hid bombs under veils and removed veils to penetrate from the Casbah, or Arab quarter, into the French quarter (*Dying* 33). The prerevolutionary moment constituted a period during which the European dreamed of unveiling and controlling an Algerian feminine. During the revolutionary period the veil's removal, a form of Algerian mimicry of the French, is characterized in terms of the penetration and intermingling of "French" and "Arab" space that takes place as the "veil" separating the Arab quarter of the "Kasbah" is removed to reveal the symbolic contact of Western and Algerian spheres that will characterize Algeria during the period of decolonization: "The protective mantle of the Kasbah, the almost organic curtain of security that the Arab city weaves around the native is withdrawn, and the uncovered Algerian woman is launched in the city of the conqueror" (*Dying* 32). The Algerian use of unveiling as a tactic of camouflage constitutes a movement toward a properly "decolonized" conception of space and culture. Of course we know that this has not necessarily occurred in Algeria, where the veil takes on contested significations according to political and personal preferences. However, what is crucial here is the way that Berkane's spectatorship of Algerian space within the Casbah as a feminine space to be unveiled by a masculine gaze suggests a return to colonial conceptions of space, gender, sight, and national territory.[11] This masculinist, retrograde perspective is evident when the narrator, discussing the voyeuristic quality of the street, remarks, "Tant de fois, il aimait se perdre dans cette cohue d'homme lourds, dans ce magma d'odeurs . . . tant de fois dans l'exil, ensuite il s'est imaginé que le microcosme de cet univers passé garderait à jamais sa réalité, mais dans quels lieux intacts?" (So many times, he loved getting lost in this mass of heavy men, in this magma of odors . . . later, in exile, so many times he imagined the microcosm of this past universe would keep its reality forever, but in what places intact?) (70). This desire for stasis is linked not only to a feminized presence but also to a maternal one that haunts Berkane and ultimately distances him from the present. This desire for territory as an unchanging and feminine space evokes a colonialist ideology, whereby place is at once rendered familiar and controllable through reference to a maternal and feminized space of conquest. Ultimately, the masculinist gaze evoked by Berkane that penetrates the streets of the Casbah functions as a desired static viewpoint, a perspective steeped in the violence of a colonial past. Like the colonial perspective seeking an authentic "feminine" Algeria as victim of its gaze, Berkane too seeks refuge in a similar territorialist desire. Berkane's diasporic past and exile from his "homeland," which are experiences inflected by colonialism, contribute to his vision of contemporary Algeria. Such a vision remains victim of the colonial optic in its mimicry.

Referring to the photos of the Algerian landscape that he has developed, Berkane remarks that he feels distanced from the experience of the present, unable to live his return fully: "je n'en reviens pas d'être là; de retour. Vraiment? Je suis tout à fait là?" (I can't believe I am here; back again. Truly? Am I really completely here?) (35). This perceived estrangement is linked to a feminization of topography and of language, a return to an eternal, maternal presence that would infuse Berkane's view of the landscape: "La voix qui interroge en moi vogue des mots français à ceux de ma mère . . . elle vacille, hésite d'une langue à l'autre, d'une rive à l'autre: ma mère en moi s'étonne, ses yeux m'interrogeant. Ce jeu muet m'habite. En vérité, en cet espace, et la mer devant moi . . . je vis ma solitude comme un cadeau" (The voice in me that questions moves from French to the language of my Mother . . . it vacillates, hesitates from one language to the other, from one shore to the other: my mother in me is astonished, her eyes interrogate me. This mute game inhabits me. To tell the truth, in this space, with the sea before me . . . I live my solitude as a present) (35). Berkane's vision of space is inflected by a maternal presence, one that finds the mère/mer homophony, or mother/sea proximity in spoken French, creating a retrograde, immobile vision in Berkane.[12] This vision is one that interrogates the multilingual, multicultural shifting between French and Arabic, and instead returns to the mother tongue and its singular conception of territory. Like a fetus returned to a womb, Berkane is unable to react to the present circumstances of his current life or the conditions of contemporary Algeria. It is as if he is cradled in the embryonic fluid of the mother sea upon which he gazes, a maternal presence that returns him to a childlike state, a period of time akin not only to his days in the incipient nation of Algeria at the time of the Algerian War of Independence but also to the childlike state of the Algerian nation itself. Berkane thus characterizes his return to Algeria as a "retour aride," where he is plagued by what he refers to as "mon immobilité" (my immobility) (86). This immobility is profoundly linked to the way he sees his surroundings only as distant remnants of the colonial era and of loss. Of the Casbah he remarks, "Et ces lieux réoccupés semblent, je ne sais pourquoi (ou simplement sous mon regard aigu d'enfant qui se ressouvient du quartier), oui, ces lieux, autrefois réservés aux petits Blancs, semblent encore attendre ces derniers" (And these reoccupied places seem, I don't know why [or simply because of my acute childhood gaze that remembers this neighborhood], yes, these places, otherwise reserved for the French colonizers, still seem to be waiting for them) (86). The neighborhood sites look out at Berkane as if "d'une autre rive" (from another shore) and appear "en images désolées de manège" (in sad carnival images) (85). Although Berkane can clearly see that the inhabitants of the Casbah are victims of a "laisser-aller collectif" (collective resignation), his vision of Algeria, distanced from the present and conditioned by its images of colonial-era loss and desolation, precludes him from engagement and ultimately leads him to complicity with other victims of this past that will not pass.

Additionally, colonial history is presented to Berkane's eyes in the form of a cinematographic aesthetic, an aesthetic that will be linked to a form of colonial imprisonment. Awakened from a sleep wherein he dreams of a French butcher tortured before his shop, Berkane "fait redérouler le rêve, scène après scène: tranche de la vie lointaine qui s'étire" (replays the dream, scene by scene: slice of distant life that stretches out) (40). Described in this way, the memory of the scene takes on the visual quality of a scene from a film — replayed, repeated, *déjà vu*. Moreover, the scene is perceived through "une trouée" (a hole) and takes place inside "un grand cercle" (a large circle) of spectators (41). Berkane "revoit le corps du boucher, cette fois de dos et en l'air [. . .] Revient l'image choc du rêve: des jambes courtes, de dos, gigotant dans l'espace, là-haut, au dessus du petit Berkane au regard épouvanté" (sees again the butcher's body, this time from the back, and in the air [. . .] The shocking image of the dream reappears: short legs, from the back, wriggling in space up there, above little Berkane with the horrified look) (40). This scene of victimization will accompany Berkane on his walk in the Casbah, and its spectral quality linked to the colonial period — its cinematic quality — will reappear when Berkane attempts to discover what is new in the neighborhood of his childhood.

While walking on Rue du Regard, Berkane follows a path leading to the cinéma Nedjma and then to a shop beside the Rue des Bouchers (72). The Nedjma cinema and Butcher's Street recall events from the colonial period, and, of course, evoke the scene of the butcher's shop replayed and described by Berkane above.[13] Moreover, these two places serve as memory sites, monuments that represent colonial aesthetics and drama as much as the path, the street, that leads us into the past. Here as elsewhere, Berkane becomes a victim of the memory and the aesthetics of the war, lost in the images of a past that separates him from the contemporary Casbah that holds him prisoner of its structure.

This imprisonment in the past is illustrated when the narrator defines these images as "une scène primitive" (a primal scene) and informs us that Berkane "s'est oublié dans ce passé d'images mortes" (has forgotten himself in this past of dead images) (46, 76). Furthermore, when Berkane prepares to enter the Casbah, it is described as a human having the quality of a haunted house: "La Casbah va lui proposer ses venelles, ses ruelles en nœuds, en escaliers d'ombre — 'ombre sans mystère'" (The Casbah will offer to him her alleyways, her backstreets knotted with stairways of shadow — "shadow without mystery") (68). The known quality of these shadows suggests the spectral aspect of the past — that which returns, that which haunts. Additionally, the labyrinthine backstreets of the Casbah tend to suggest the familiar, the past, thus creating a place that can be experienced only through the colonial period. Adopting a Rimbaldien tone, Berkane points out how much he is victim of a poetic nostalgia for the Casbah when he notes, "O ma Casbah, mon navire" (O my Casbah, my ship) (83). Berkane abandons himself to a poetic wandering out of his control, which leads ceaselessly, wave after wave, toward the colonial past.

Thus, *La Disparition de la langue française* is a "casbah novel,"[14] which makes of the subject a victim of colonial memories, memories that distance him from the present and position his existence in a non-place, which is not that of the postcolonial nomad of Deleuze and Guattari, whose existence would be defined by movement and the freedom to create and recreate his identity as nomadic hero (*Mille* 329–30). Caught in the trap of the memory of a Parisian lover left on the other side, at once free and imprisoned in the structure of the Casbah, Berkane recalls Pépé, hero of Duvivier's film. The novel replays the colonial film through a cinematographic writing that emphasizes the fascination for the labyrinthine visual structure of the Casbah. Like Pépé, who knows intimately the spatial structure of the Casbah, Berkane becomes prisoner of the colonial structure of the memory that divides France and Algeria, and the people of Algeria.[15] In this sense we must recall that the novel is set in 1991. The turn to fundamentalist violence after the elections divided Algeria into a nation that had to side with a purist version of Algeria, untainted by the West, or a menaced populace that believed in the possibility of cultural pluralism and openness to Western culture and the French language. The 1991 setting is not simply arbitrary here; it is intended to mark the beginning of a period of intense terror and victimization in Algeria, a civil war that took the form of colonial-era warfare and that pitted Algeria against the Western presence of the French. Berkane's immersion in the sites and sensations of colonial Algeria and its revolutionary ferment place him within the haunting cycle of the 1991 return to Manichean colonial divisions separating Algeria and the West. The novel plays on the colonial intertext of Duvivier in that Berkane, divided between two countries due to a history of crime and victimization (colonialism), is unable (as is Pépé le Moko) to leave this colonial aesthetic, these Manichean divisions that continue to haunt Algeria.[16]

The novel replays Duvivier's colonial film, placing the entire scope of the film in the postcolonial context in Algeria when Berkane disappears at the end of the novel. Although he searches for the place where he had been imprisoned and tortured during the Algerian War due to insurrectional euphoria, Berkane disappears and, like Pépé, becomes a perpetual prisoner of the colonial past. This euphoria is denounced in the text when Berkane tells us that he imagines himself "en héros, en meneur ou, plus modestement, en manifestant de première ligne, mais tombant, les mains et la poitrine nues, devant les soldats (comme si je voulais savourer, post mortem, à partir du paradis musulman des martyrs, ma propre gloire!)" (as a hero, a leader, or more modestly, a front-line protester, but falling, bare hands and chest, before the soldiers, as if I wanted to savor postmortem, through the Muslim martyrs' paradise, my own glory!) (210). Although not explicitly naming those who are guilty in his disappearance, the novel leads us to believe that Berkane disappears at the hands of fundamentalists, but his disappearance is also due to his desire to see the sites of his so-called heroism again. The reversal of naïve heroism — the naïve glance that imagines it can revise such a past in the postcolonial light in Algeria — leads to an even more naïve victimization.

Although he leaves the labyrinthine structure of the Casbah at the end of the text, Berkane is not victorious as was Theseus when he exited the labyrinth. He becomes a specter of the colonial violence of the Casbah, and remains in many ways the victim of his self-investment in the colonial past. His body and his existence remain suspended at the end of the text, aligned with a postcolonial non-place.[17] This suspension reflects, in a much larger sense, the civil war, the destruction and loss in Algeria, which stem from a repetition of the Algerian War in the form of a civil war. This return of history in another form would erase all trace of cultural difference, all memory of a colonial presence, but ends up only reinscribing the memory of that past, as is suggested by the title of the novel *La Disparition de la langue française*. Moreover, this erasure of difference is suggested by Berkane's search for the grotto or cave where he had been tortured by the French. This site reminds us of Plato's cave and the origins of the aesthetic "de la trace et de la différence" (of the trace and of difference), be they linguistic, cultural, or other (Derrida, *L'écriture* 45). The fact that the search for this site leads to Berkane's disappearance at the hands of those who wanted to destroy difference suggests the erasure of any trace, of any difference in Algeria. This situation thus reflects the political context of fundamentalism in Algeria that would erase the traces of occidental presence and of difference. Djebar's novel demonstrates that this cultural climate is not motivated by religious affiliation and a draconian adherence to dogma, but rather by a desire for territorialism, an impetus to reoccupy the sites of former Western invasion and occupation.[18]

With the references to Duvivier's film, Djebar emphasizes the difficulty of emerging from the spatial, mnemonic, and aesthetic structure of colonialism represented by the Casbah in Algeria. The theme of imprisonment, on the formal level, can be understood through the way the novel, taken with its intertext *Pépé le Moko*, is transformed into a labyrinth. That is, the colonial images that haunt the text function as a means of suspending the attempt to reimagine existence in Algeria since the mythic victory over the labyrinth would signify an imprisonment in the ideology of hero and victim.

Djebar's text underscores the centrality of this relationship between spectatorship, (post)colonial victimization, and the genesis of postcolonial narrative in its attention to the coincidence of Berkane's disappearance and the incomplete narrative he ultimately leaves behind. Suspension of postcolonial existence in Algeria, defined by its relationship to colonial victimization, is emphasized by the autobiographical text entitled *L'Adolescent*, which Berkane is writing at the time of his disappearance. Motivated by the desire to end the composition of the story of his adolescence characterized by "une effervescence toute romantique" (a completely romantic effervescence) (210), Berkane searches for the site of his adolescent prison from the colonial period. The text shows us that such a desire to recuperate or to close the temporality of existence lived during the insurrection is only an illusion. With the story Berkane is writing, Djebar emphasizes the link between the aesthetics of language and of the gaze (the idea of seeing his native country again, and of reconceiving his existence), and Algerian subjectivity in its attempts to imagine postcolonial existence in Algeria.

Berkane is successful in neither his return nor his story since his attempts take as a starting point the idea that one might return and reconstitute existence fragmented by colonial victimization through the imagination or a story that begins with insurrectional and national euphoria. Such a narrative cannot end in a postcolonial subjectivity without violence, without loss, for such an appropriation of the past is inspired by a territorial and nationalist violence similar to that of colonialism. What prevents Berkane from envisioning his country otherwise is the quest for a story that will allow him to put down roots, to close the temporality of his past in Algeria. In this way the text shows us that in order to envision his subjectivity in other ways, the Algerian subject must part with the ideology that wants at all cost to root its national history in a space that would be purely "Algerian." Djebar puts language at the center of this question. For the Algerian subject who wants to see again and narrate his existence in the postcolonial light, *La Disparition de la langue française* shows the necessity to accept the fragmentation, pluralism, and polyvalence of existence in Algeria.[19] Such a story cannot take root so as to pronounce a singular national history and, consequently, to overtake national memory. It is only in accepting — without excusing — negation and the fractured and fragmented story of existence that colonialism and its insurrection offer that one can leave behind the ideology of victimization and of heroism of the formerly colonized nation. Victimization and heroism in Algeria, as Djebar shows, are both part of a similar ideology in their commemorative tendencies that remain based upon the violent history of the victim's position and a subsequent legacy of appropriating that narrative. But awareness of the fractured nature of postcolonial existence does not suffice either, for the text suggests that the desire for an aesthetics of violence, the desire to see, and see again — hence the importance of Duvivier's colonial intertext — leads to a repetition, or even to a dangerous commemoration of the colonial conflict. Here, the concept of spectatorship of terrorism and victimization completes Djebar's account. Berkane's comments just before his disappearance reinforce such a warning: "maintenant que je suis rentré, est-ce que le martyre va reprendre: les convulsions, la folie, le silence? Serais-je rentré pour rester, comme autrefois, à regarder: regarder et me déchirer?" (now that I've returned, will the martyr take over again: convulsions, madness, silence? Will I have returned to stand, as before, watching: watching and tearing myself apart?) (242). Here, watching and acting constitute identical gestures, for all active intervention serves to perpetuate the aesthetics of war.

The text shows that the only means of combating the appropriation of any movement by this vicious circle is to negate the conventional idea of the hero. The true hero of the novel is therefore a negative hero, for he escapes appropriation by the state and by the actors of a war that perpetuates the memory of foundational violence. Citing Bertolt Brecht, who himself proposed a negative aesthetics of distanciation, Rachid, a friend of Berkane, notes: "Malheureux, le pays qui a besoin d'un héros, n'est-ce pas?" (The country that needs a hero is miserable, isn't it?) (100). Rachid continues, making references to the fundamentalist heroes who appear as mimic men of the colonial war: "Les héros, en Algérie, pendant la guerre, on les a appelés les moudjahiddin, un terme religieux, n'est-ce pas?"

(The heroes in Algeria during the war were called moudjahiddin, a religious term, right?) (100). The text suggests that critical distancing, a negation of the ideology of the hero must take place to combat the extremism that creates heroes and victims. Thus, Berkane says that "le héros pur et nu" (the pure unadorned hero) of his childhood was his uncle Tchaida, a drug addict "considéré comme le dernier des derniers" (considered the last of a dying breed) (105). Howling in his neighborhood after curfew, asking the people to forgive his behavior, Tchaida was killed in the street by a "zouave" officer in the company of a Frenchman (104). According to Berkane, "ce héros malheureux, vulnérable [est] le seul innocent — pas le héros politique, ni même celui du nationalisme: non, en quelque sorte, le héros absolu, lui qui nous a fait, à l'avance ses adieux!" (This miserable, vulnerable hero [is] the only innocent one — not the political hero, nor even the nationalist: no, in a way, the absolute hero, the one who said his goodbyes in advance) (105). If the text seems to represent Tchaida, the crazy drug addict as absolute hero, it is because his image as loser and madman cannot return to haunt under the national ideology of the state. His image escapes the politics of commemoration of hero and victim led by the state, and refuses the place of colonial memory. Tchaida's "goodbyes in advance" represent the refusal of a return after his death. The spectral image of the martyr of colonial victimization cannot be appropriated by the national politics of fundamentalism in its attempts to rid the nation of all difference. Tchaida's madness remains lucidity in comparison to this other madness.

The denunciation of the creation of hero and victim and of their capacity to return to haunt the former colony is common in Djebar's work. The reexamination of the appropriation of the heroic figure of the martyr was already evident in her novel *La Femme sans sépulture*, which preceded *La Disparition*. In both texts Djebar denounces the politics that appropriate the image of the hero of the colonial past while praising the nation as perpetual victim. In these two recent novels Djebar emphasizes the problematic of aesthetics by spotlighting the explicit visual staging of the colonial past, of the quest for a form of representation that could recount colonial history without becoming a victim of this history in its contemporary incarnations.

In many ways Djebar's novel, although clearly set within the postcolony of Algeria, offers a critique of the ideology of heroism and victimization that we have seen in Bouchareb's *Indigènes*. The novel demonstrates that commemoration of the colonial-era victim and hero is predicated upon the very concept of the nation. In the case of *Indigènes* we have seen that commemoration of the colonial-era hero is organized around a certain fetishism of French national space and identity. In *La Disparition de la langue française* a similar national fetishism is in place, only with respect to Algeria. Djebar's text demonstrates that an attempt to envision postcolonial politics from the perspective of the colonial-era victim-hero paradigm frequently leads to a fetishistic relationship to the nation that is unable to view postcolonial place from the perspective of its current terror, a terror frequently related to the persistent problems of extreme nationalism rooted in a colonial lexicon.

The reexamination of the appropriation of the martyr by political aesthetics is also evident in *La Disparition de la langue française* when Amar, a childhood friend of Berkane, says to him: "Tu as parlé de nos héros, quant aux monuments aux morts dressés face à la demeure de l'architecte Pouillon: si nos martyrs ressuscitaient, beaucoup d'entre eux hésiteraient, je pense, à se sacrifier de nouveau, tu sais pourquoi? [. . .] — À cause de tant de laideur qui est censée les honorer!" (You spoke of our heroes, regarding the monuments to the dead erected across from the home of the architect Pouillon: if our martyrs came back to life, many of them would hesitate, I think, to sacrifice themselves again, do you know why? [. . .] — Because of so much ugliness intended to honor them!) (81). Here, ideology, the aesthetics of the hero-victim that make the nation a victim of a "past that will not pass," serves only to establish the specters of conflict (Rousso and Conan 3).

Djebar's use of Duvivier's *Pépé le Moko* as a central intertextual reference in *La Disparition de la langue française* is crucial to the novel's experiment and consequent indictment of the ideology of victimization. Djebar's attempt to map Duvivier's colonial-era film into a postcolonial narrative serves as a unique experiment, one that plays on the reflection of a criminal history begun in the West and relocated in Algeria. In the novel's attempt to generate a new narrative from the repetitive history of colonial-era crime translated into Algeria's contemporary history of terror, Djebar plays on the very fusion and reflection of narratives of both Western and non-Western origin. In a larger sense this constitutes an investigation into whether the history of crime that both narratives share, transported both spatially and temporally, might enable a new narrative. Djebar's text suggests that the victimization, which is central, although not materially and visually present, to such narratives, ultimately vitiates the attempt to see differently and, consequently, to generate new postcolonial narratives untainted by the cyclical violence of colonial history. In cinematographic terms Djebar's text demonstrates how narratives of victimization are often analogous to visual mappings of the colonial experience of victimization. They reinforce one another and establish modes of spectatorship that, even in their novelty and experimentation, often return us to an incestuous vision of violence and victimization shared by the West and non-West alike.

Conclusion

Alejandro González Iñárritu's internationally acclaimed film *Babel* (2006), starring Brad Pitt and Cate Blanchett, begins in the Moroccan desert with a troubled young American couple, Richard and Susan, traveling on a tourist bus. At this point, despite the different settings and epochs, the scene is uncannily reminiscent of the beginning of Albert Camus's 1957 short story *The Adulterous Woman*, which begins with a troubled young French couple, Janine and Marcel, traveling on a bus through the Algerian desert. What unites the colonial-era short story and Iñárritu's film, though, are the remnants of colonial vision that inform the way the North African context is viewed by the outside Western gaze as a confusing and dangerous setting, where the Western viewer might impose his or her cultural vision of the landscape.[1]

As the tourist bus carrying the American couple winds itself through the Moroccan desert, two young Moroccan boys carelessly take aim at the road below with their father's rifle, and with no intentional malice, accidentally hit the passing bus. The boys were carelessly testing the rifle, which is kept to protect the family's herd of sheep, from atop a steep hill.[2] As the camera cuts to the inside of the bus, we learn through a delayed reaction that Susan has become victim of the boy's wounding bullet. As attempts are made to aid the American and secure her evacuation from the remote location, international media coverage begins, grossly deforming the incident. The focus of media speculation quickly turns to terrorism. We learn, too, that in keeping with the film's title, the confusing Moroccan event and landscape become translated into a common yet divisive language of terrorism shared by the international community. However, in this symbolism of international unity, the film demonstrates a larger cultural dispersal of humankind, a "clash of civilizations" between the Arab setting of North Africa and the external "Western" world based upon a shared utter misunderstanding. This geopolitical Babel, characterized by the dispersion and misunderstanding of the international community, although at first glance seemingly removed from reference to colonial history, might be seen as a product of colonial vision and cultural imperialism on the part of the Western viewer and victim.

Like Janine and Marcel in Camus's short story, the American couple is a symbol of Western cultural imperialism traveling seemingly carefree through the North African desert before the puncturing shot.[3] This wounding shot, which draws the Western media focus to the imagined terror of North Africa, enacts a return of colonial history where the Western viewpoint falls victim to the stereotypical motif of the dangerous North African context. As in the history of colonial relations, the wounding recognition of lurking danger is central to the Western vision of the North African backdrop in the film.

The return of colonial history, I will argue, although not explicitly referenced in *Babel*, is symbolically represented in the victimizing shot of the American traveler and its interpretation. For Roland Barthes the framed image is characterized by a piercing yet delayed recognition in the form of the *punctum*. According to Barthes, the *punctum* is a point of recognition — a return of memory at first unlocatable — that is etched onto the body of the viewer. For Barthes, this point of memory pierces the viewer because it recalls another time frame, a haunting image.[4] The *punctum* introduces a spectral presence into the viewing framework — a temporality that is incongruous with the present yet very much a part of it. In *Babel* the delayed wounding that reverberates around the international viewing community recalls another time frame, the haunting presence of colonial history embedded in the visual and cultural perspective the West adopts in relation to North Africa. The Western world — represented by the media representations of the accident — adopts the piercing shot as its own wound and occupies the position of victim in the symbolic presence it shares with the wounded couple. What ensues from this wounding presence, characterized by the themes of Western imperialism, is an understanding of terrorism based on the victim's position and on a historically inflected vision of the "clash" of Western and Arab worlds. The *punctum* in *Babel*, we might say, serves as the historical overlap between terrorism and colonial history. As a victimizing wound, the *punctum* represents the embedded nature of historical moments. It is also very much related to spectatorship and its memory of trauma.[5]

In the previous chapters of this book, I have attempted to demonstrate how the victim's position, what we might call a *punctum* or wounding presence, serves to inform the relationship between colonial history and our contemporary age of terror. In certain films examined here, like *The Battle of Algiers*, the focus on this position within our contemporary age of terror suggests the current drive to shape and appropriate the image of the victim's position so as to better occupy the position of victimizer. In other instances, as in Haneke's film *Caché*, colonial-era history returns with a vengeance, suggesting the ways the spectacle of victimization establishes a piercing, indeed cutting, perspective within the contemporary context. What is at issue in all the works examined in the preceding pages is the nature of the return of colonial history and the problematic position of the victim. The argument I have attempted to make throughout this book is that an insistent focus on victimization from colonial history proves to be a dangerous and potentially wounding point of identification in the age of terror. Although the works I have examined speak to issues of spectatorship directly related to postcolonial cinema, they also speak to the larger context of ways of viewing and situating colonial history and the position of the victim within our contemporary context. They suggest that the victim's position within the history of imperialism is central to understanding how certain forms of terror and resistance to them function today. Ultimately, all of the works represented here demonstrate how the North African context remains an exemplary case for the age of terror given the numerous returns of colonial history it provides and the ensuing tensions between the West and an Arab world that those returns signal. Deeply rooted wounds linked to the history of colonialism in North Africa remain unhealed. The works in this book ask how to view them and how they are viewed today.

The setting of North Africa for a film like *Babel* that treats terrorism is not a surprising choice. North Africa often serves as a focal point for the fascination with terrorism. Barbet Shroeder's recent award-winning documentary, *L'Avocat de la terreur, Terror's Advocate* (2007), is a fitting example of how North Africa and its colonial history play into the vision of the contemporary matrix of terrorism.[6] Schroeder's documentary follows the career of the controversial attorney Jacques Vergès, who defended Djamila Bouhired, known as "la Pasionaria," the freedom fighter during the Algerian War who was sentenced to death for planting bombs in Algerian cafés where high concentrations of French colonizers congregated. Vergès obtained Bouhired's release and subsequently married her. In the wake of September 11, the discussion of Vergès's courtroom defense of an Algerian bomber during the French occupation of that country raises questions as to whether avowed terrorists and mass murderers who do not deny their crimes deserve a "fair" defense. It also raises the question as to where we draw the line — or how we draw a line — between "terrorist" and "freedom fighter." Moreover, Schroeder's portrayal of Vergès raises the question as to how we might draw the line between Vergès as victim or victimizer, upholder of international justice or terrorist. Further, the documentary creates a crisis regarding the very definition of these terms.

Although the documentary treats Vergès's highly controversial defense of terrorists such as Magdalena Kopp, Carlos the Jackal, the Holocaust denier Roger Garaudy, and the Gestapo chief Klaus Barbie, the documentary's focus and title reflect Vergès's role on both sides of the perceived victim/victimizer position.[7] We are brought to see his defense of guerilla warfare in the armed struggle for independence in Algeria against the French colonizer and his defense of icons of imperialist oppression such as Klaus Barbie. Yet, Schroeder begins the documentary with the history of Algerian independence and the defense of terrorism as an anticolonial stance. Schroeder's documentary places the question of colonial-era victimization in North Africa at the center of the web of known terrorist history. In so doing the documentary illustrates how deeply related the issue of perspective on that form of victimization and terrorism from colonial history is to other international forms of terrorism. Moreover, I would argue that the success of the documentary is related to the way it forces the viewer, through its portrayal of Vergès as an equal opportunity defender, to see the way that the very position of victim or victimizer in relation to terror is relative. It creates an uncomfortable position for the viewer, who is forced to see that the role of victim in relation to terrorism may very well be relative and interchangeable, depending on the perspective adopted.

The works examined in this book illustrate that the victim's position must be projected carefully within the age of terror, for it is frequently subject to appropriation or accommodation by the memorial gesture. Set in France during the struggle for Algerian independence, Thomas Gilou's popular film *Michou d'Auber* (2007) starring Gérard Depardieu and Nathalie Baye, provides a compelling example of how the memorial gesture might accommodate issues of colonial-era victimization without ever fully addressing their genesis and operation within the contemporary context. The film centers on the adoption of an Algerian boy, Messaoud (Samy Seghir), by a French couple Georges and Gisèle, played by Depardieu and Baye. Messaoud is given up for adoption when his mother becomes terminally ill and his father, who works long hours in a factory, can no longer care for him. Messaoud is given the name Michel and the nickname Michou, and his identity as an Algerian is hidden by Gisèle from her ex-army Gaullist husband, Georges. The events of the Algerian War serve as the background for the film, while the principal focus remains on the relationship between Michou and his adoptive parents, whose relationship Michou's very presence manages to salvage.[8]

Michou d'Auber, like Bouchareb's *Indigènes*, is an example of a return of North African colonial history focused on an accommodation. Like Bouchareb's film, Gilou's portrayal of colonial history overlooks the vagaries of torture and victimization that were a part of the Algerian War on both sides. However, it is a film that also overlooks the relationship of contemporary discourses of oppression in France rooted in colonial history, such as those examined in the second chapter. On one hand, *Michou d'Auber* seems focused on the imperative of accommodating one of the genealogies of North African colonial history in France. On the other, we might say that it completely elides questions of torture, victimization, and their relationship to the contemporary context of Muslim populations and their place within the French nation. Although *Michou d'Auber* avoids the problematic position of allowing colonial history and its stories of victimization to haunt its screen, it does not examine what it might truly mean to accommodate that history in France.

I have frequently criticized or identified a problematic focus on victimization from colonial history in the works examined in the preceding pages. However, I have also pointed to the way that films — and the use of films — productively accommodate victimization from a critical perspective by pointing to the ways it produces a haunting spectacle or a contest over the ideological territory of the victim. Most importantly, the films examined in this work all demonstrate that victimization is central to the way we see and create terror. Imperialist history, like a moment of time out of joint that haunts our contemporary landscape, remains intricately connected to the questions of terror posed today.[9] The works examined in this book all suggest that whether we choose to adopt or renounce the victim's position from the long history of imperialism may very well define our answers to those questions.

Notes

INTRODUCTION

1. The essays assembled by Nayan Chanda and Strobe Talbott in the volume *The Age of Terror* rely upon the same phrase. Although the collection looks critically upon the idea of America as the fulcrum for the idea of the "age of terror," it nonetheless centers its analysis on the United States. My focus in this book is not the United States, and the perspective I adopt targets the intersection of France and North Africa, in particular, Algeria. My use of the phrase the age of terror has a broader base than its use in the collection of essays assembled by Chanda and Talbott. I attempt to distance the phrase from any one national perspective. Instead, my intention is to demonstrate how the dynamics of victimization in relationship to colonial history are a large component of contemporary terror and frequently find themselves in direct relationship to their diverse incarnations. Although my focus here is more on the relationships between France and its former colonies, my central argument concerning the space of the victim as central to the dynamics of terror can be seen to have direct implications in the larger post–9/11 climate.

2. In *Culture and Imperialism* Edward Said writes of the desire to occupy or control the cultural position of the Other as a part of the underlying dynamics of imperialism: "Imperialism and the culture associated with it affirm both the primacy of geography and an ideology about the control of territory. The geographical sense makes projections — imaginative, cartographic, military, economic, historical, or in a general sense cultural" (78).

3. Postcolonial studies has widely regarded the representation of histories of colonial victimization as a salutary gesture of revisionist history designed to give voice to the formerly oppressed. Nonetheless, certain critics have warned, in different ways than this book does, of the unproblematic return of colonial history. Gayatri Spivak is arguably the most adamant concerning the vicissitudes of resurrecting the occulted colonial subject of history and advises the historian against viewing the subaltern as "object" of study (Spivak and Gunew). Spivak echoes Robert Young who signals "the hidden ways in which nominally radical, or oppositional historians and often unknowingly, or even knowingly, perpetuate the structures and presuppositions of the very systems which they oppose" (*Colonial Desire* 161–62). The haunting temporality of colonialism, however,

frequently returns to trouble even those endeavors with the best intentions. My argument is that the focus on victimization in the return of colonial history in the age of terror is informed by a haunting territorialism that is central to the terrorist's imaginary — a desire to occupy the territory of the victim.

4. If Huntington's work has become popular in the wake of September 11, it is perhaps because of its division of the West and "the rest" into competing categories that play upon the very threat of victimization. Said's article "The Clash of Ignorance" argues that Huntington's characterization of fixed "civilizations" is predicated upon the fictitious assumption that each civilization is self-enclosed and structured by the idea of maintaining a clash or wartime status. Although Said does not use the term victimization, his critique of Huntington's conception of the geopolitical landscape as a way of viewing the world map aligns with my discussion of the role of victimization as an organizing structure in the age of terror.

5. Bernard Lewis's article "The Roots of Muslim Rage" is emblematic of the way Huntington's formula has been used to discuss the victimizing threats and claims commonly associated with the age of terror. See also Engin Erdem's article "The Clash of Civilizations."

6. See Fernando Solanas and Octavio Gettino, "Towards a Third Cinema." I also more thoroughly discuss third cinema in chapter 1.

7. As an Italian-Algerian production that appeared soon after Algerian independence, *The Battle of Algiers* represents an example of a nascent Algerian cinema. Algeria did not have much of a cinema of its own until 1957, when the FLN (Algerian Nationalist Liberation Front) established a cinema school. *The Battle of Algiers* was produced by Antonio Musu of Igor Films in Rome and coproduced by Casbah Films, a production company founded by Yacef Saadi, a leading figure of the FLN.

8. Mike Wayne remarks, "Third Cinema seeks to detach what is positive, life-affirming and critical from cinemas One and Two and give them a more expanded, socially connected articulation" (10). Wayne is concerned with the lack of a resistant edge in certain third cinema films, such as *The Battle of Algiers*, where revolutionary "commitment" is "just not very overt" (17).

9. For Ranjanna Khanna a fourth cinema would represent another category that would allow for agency for women in revolution: "A fourth cinema that moves beyond the guerilla cinema where the camera is a weapon would be a revolutionary cinema of the cocoon, where the metaphor of the birth of a nation is not repressed into a denial of the feminine. It would be a cinema that could give voice, silence, and image to women in the revolution, where the uncanny could become reified on the screen" (*Algeria Cuts* 124).

10. According to Hamid Naficy, "both accented films and Third Cinema films are historically conscious, politically engaged, critically aware, generically hybridized, and artisanally produced" (31). Naficy's identification of resistance in third and accented cinema, which seeks to recreate a vision of "authentic" culture in opposition to Western cultural influence, embodies one of the dangers of resistance cinema in relation to the age of terror; namely, a reproduction of a vision of culture predicated on the notion of the "clash of civilizations" and their categorization: "Third Cinema and accented cinema are alike in their attempts to define and create a nostalgic, even fetishized, authentic prior culture — before contamination by the West in the case of Third Cinema, and before displacement and emigration in the case of the accented cinema" (31). In *Postcolonial Images* Roy Armes points out that hybridity or the "accented" quality in North African cinema might both provide and preclude a form of postcolonial resistance by representing issues that might not be otherwise represented in North Africa and by avoiding issues of realism and direct confrontation with the landscape of North Africa (186). Armes's discussion of hybridity and resistance, published in 2005, makes no reference to the relationship between North African cinema and the context of terrorism today except for this allusion to the impossibility of filming the Algerian landscape directly: "But because Algeria has become inaccessible as a location for shooting, it has become a kind of phantom in the works of certain of these filmmakers" (186).

11. When, after nearly two weeks of ongoing riots had spread across much of France's marginalized urban periphery, French prime minister Dominique de Villepin issued a "state of emergency" across more than a quarter of national territory, he instated a measure derived from the 1955 colonial-era law designed to curb support for the Algerian War of Independence.

12. In my discussion of the belated nature of postcolonial theory, I am indebted to Ali Behdad's prescriptive warning that "postcolonial belatedness" can only be an effective means of intervention if it uses its historicity to critique ongoing cultural conditions that produce unequal power relations (78). Although Behdad's critique of the belated nature of postcolonial theory does not address the questions of victimization or terror, it does address the problematic return of colonial history.

13. It is interesting that the relationship between Malek Alloula's intended critique of the postcards and the "present" is overlooked to a great extent. The blunt of criticism focuses on reinscription of the images, taking for granted the prolonged existence of a colonial-era gaze. While the masculine colonial gaze is a problematic point of identification in Alloula's work, the issue seems

to run deeper, in that such identifications do not enable a critical approach to contemporary issues. Moreover, a focus on the dynamics of the colonial gaze suggests an equally problematic investment in colonial-era dynamics of power, suggesting a view of these oppressed subjects as static victims, haunting relics of a colonial scheme of victimization. For a critique of Alloula's work in terms of the problem of reinscription, see Mieke Bal; Gregory Betts; Rey Chow; Marnia Lazreg; Laura Rice-Sayer; Winifred Woodhull.

14. Young argues that the organic ebullition of this movement should serve as an example of how postcolonial consciousness might cultivate its interventionist nature in the face of neocolonial and global forms of power (ii).

15. Outlining the affective charge of two photos from colonial Algeria, Young locates "traces of the violence, defiance, struggles, and suffering of individuals, that represent the political ideas of community, equality . . . and dignity" (ix).

16. Echoing the translation of Frantz Fanon's 1959 essay, "Algeria Unveiled," which traces the Western phallic unveiling of Algerian women as it is "transformed into a technique of camouflage, into a means of struggle," Young repeats the fascinated male gaze of colonial culture mentioned by Fanon, which seeks behind the veil, in the Algerian woman's would-be sexuality, the essence and eruption of resistance (*Postcolonialism*).

17. Young's conception of the return of colonial history is based upon the idea of turning the former victim into the victimizer, the gazed upon subject into the active agent of a returning gaze.

18. Without a doubt Iain Chambers imbues this encounter with a "culturally authentic Other" with a haunting aura. The turn to a situated, authentic image of culture and resistance in postcolonial criticism is pervasive. As Peter Hallward argues, "the spectre of cultural authenticity haunts postcolonial criticism at every step" (37). A focus on the local, situated, and authentic cultural encounter traced back to the colonial era suggests the yearning for a depth model in the fragmented and uncertain environment of postmodern conditions of terror. Haunting itself seems to play into this search for historical depth and affect, providing a highly charged sense of conflict, resistance, and purpose. In this regard Fredric Jameson's characterization of the postmodern loss of historical depth and the dissolution of iconic national figures and modernist affect is particularly relevant. Jameson's now classic work *Postmodernism or the Cultural Logic of Late Capitalism* posits that such losses of depth produce a profound nostalgia for the past, or at least for the illusion of its organizing principles of depth (59). The valorization of haunting, the culturally authentic, and the situated encounter in the proliferation of colonial memory sites suggests the

search for depth models of historical authenticity and affect in the context of postmodern fragmentation and terror.

19. Although Conley doesn't discuss victimization explicitly in his work, his discussion of the relationship between torture, cinema, and the configurations of power in Rossellini's *Roma, Città Aperta* suggests that the projection of victimization is central to the projection of a certain worldview based upon territory. Moreover, his notion of cinema as a cartographic process contains the suggestion that victimization and the struggle for power within the cinematic image are inherent in film and spectatorship.

20. Algeria in particular has been dealing with a civil war where fundamentalist factions have attempted to "free" the country from the influence of Western culture. Disappearances, torture, and bombings have injured and killed thousands since the early 1990s. For more on this, see chapter 5. Both Tunisia and Algeria have been the reported sites of al-Qaeda initiatives. The 12 December 2007 bombing of a U.N. building in Algiers is one recent example of international terrorism that places North Africa at the center of contemporary discussion of terrorism.

1. RESUSCITATING *THE BATTLE OF ALGIERS*

1. According to Michael Kaufman, the idea to show the film came from the Directorate for Special Operations and Low-Intensity Conflict. The official responsible for this group stated, "Showing the film offers historical insight into the conduct of French operations in Algeria, and was intended to prompt informative discussion of the challenges faced by the French." Kaufman reported that the official "added that the discussion was lively and that more showings would probably be held."

2. Gillo Pontecorvo points out that no documentary footage was used in making the film. With few exceptions the actors sought out were nonprofessionals who had not participated in the events depicted in the film.

3. Stated in the Criterion Collection interview.

4. On Pontecorvo's political engagement as a filmmaker, see Carlo Celli's *Gillo Pontecorvo*.

5. Robert Stam and Louis Spence suggest that traditional representations of the racialized Other in cinema are predicated upon a spectatorial position where cinematic identification with the Other can only take place through his or her surveillance. My point is not to unfairly criticize Stam and Spence through a strawman argument, but rather to demonstrate how the resistant quality of third cinema often hinges upon the point through which spectatorial

identification takes place. Moreover, the U.S. screening of the film, as I argue below, demonstrates the policing or reinforcement of the Western strategy of surveillance of the Arab.

6. The French use of force in Algeria did, however, cause a great deal of political scandal that has traumatized political life in France. At the heart of these scandals lies the question of the French use of torture and the way it caused the Algerian nationalist cause to be viewed throughout the world. The U.S. use of torture in Iraq and with other presumed terrorists presents an analogous case that raises the question of the merits of embroiling the United States in political scandal on the geopolitical scene.

7. It is important to note that in many ways the "clash of civilizations" evident in *The Battle of Algiers* is structured by many of the same ideologies that contribute to the contemporary clash of civilizations. The problem is that the responsibility of the West and its vision of these ideologies are completely occluded in the Pentagon screening.

8. In Dipesh Chakrabarty's theorization of the status of historicity as serial time, one finds a suggestion about the invisibility of disjunctures in the writing of history by the West: "Thus the writing of history must implicitly assume a plurality of times existing together, a disjuncture of the present with itself" (109). "Making visible this disjuncture," according to Chakrabarty, is the first step in revealing the Western elision of its own vision and control of the historical narrative. The Pentagon appropriation of victimization and elision of the full narrative of colonial history in its positioning of *The Battle of Algiers* as a historical narrative analogous to the Iraqi situation aligns with Chakrabarty's conception of the Western appropriation of the historical narrative in its disavowal of temporal disjuncture.

9. Important postcolonial accounts of the Western national imaginary focus on the "disruptive" dynamics that the representation of colonial history provides in its challenge to the West. Homi Bhabha's conception of the way the "homogeneity" of national time is splintered by the time of colonialism, or by the representation of minority or resistance narratives, is emblematic of the larger postcolonial revisionist perspective. The Pentagon screening of Pontecorvo's film proved to be an event that demonstrated how the representation of the time of colonialism within the confines of the Western imaginary might also serve to reinforce the conception of the temporal and spatial boundaries of sovereignty in the West.

10. The newsreel-style footage of presumed terrorists in the film could be said to resonate with much of the newsreel images one finds in U.S. reporting

on Iraq. This similarity can be seen to establish another point of cinematic identification for U.S. spectators.

11. In *The Age of the World Target* Chow argues that self-referentiality is central to the U.S. targeting of populations that are deemed Other, and ultimately to the establishment of U.S. hegemony on the world scene. Chow points out that the self-referentiality found in American political praxis is accompanied by its reflection in the production of knowledge. Although she does not discuss the self-referentiality of surveillance in her work, the scene of Pontecorvo's work suggests similar dynamics in the production of knowledge and of Western hegemonic practices.

12. One of the real life women bombers was Zohra Drif, who became a parliamentarian in Algeria after independence from the French. She was a law student at Algiers University and the daughter of an Islamic judge. During World War II her parents told her that the occupation of France by Nazi Germany was God's revenge on the French for their treatment of Muslims. On this topic, see Louis Proyect's article "Looking Back at *The Battle of Algiers*."

13. As Michael Chanan points out, "The Argentineans suggest a position in which, to fulfill the criteria of Third Cinema, there can be nothing in political terms which is tentative or hypothetical about the content or signification of the images concerned; whereas the avant-garde or underground notion of experimentalism defends the notion of a space which is untouched by these considerations (without thereby becoming reactionary)" ("Changing" 373). Chanan's conception of the "changing geography of third cinema" suggests that the marginal and interstitial spaces from which postcolonial artists might produce today could intersect in a form of resistant solidarity. The extension of my argument about the appropriation of Pontecorvo's work is that the new post–cold war order might, at times, easily absorb such forms of resistance through an appropriation of the space of the victim.

14. For Khanna the melancholic yet persistent tones of postcolonial texts and theories point toward a continuing and hopeful exchange within the present. Where some find failure, Khanna identifies a persistent demand for justice: "Rather, I would propose, the case of Algeria, and more specifically Algiers, becomes exemplary because a certain form of sovereignty was played out which systematically engendered a melancholic remainder. It is within the affect initiated by this remainder that one could, perhaps, find a specter calling for justice. These melancholic specters, available to us only by listening to the often unspoken demands of a text, point the way toward a different future, and are profoundly material" ("Post-Palliative"). While it is difficult to see

how the specific melancholic and victimized positions identified by Khanna might truly serve as the basis for postcolonial political praxis, her sense of the insistence of the postcolonial narrative, even in failure, is suggestive for the return of Pontecorvo's masterpiece.

2. MAPPING NATIONAL IDENTITY

1. For Henry Rousso the period of "le miroir brisé" is a period when the overlooked or repressed moments of World War II history come back with a vengeance to force a reconsideration of the image of national unity. In my analysis *Indigènes* both shatters and reassembles the image of union related to this part of colonial World War II history, in that it at once portrays this overlooked or repressed part of World War II history while aspiring to an image of union through the inclusion of these North African soldiers within the narrative of French national identity.

2. The film's portrayal of the soldiers' simultaneous inclusion and exclusion from the French national narrative was, as Elizabeth Ezra has so cogently argued in *The Colonial Unconscious*, a function of the larger double bind of colonial discourse that foreclosed the possibility of the very assimilation of colonized subjects that it invited.

3. As Carrie Tarr points out, "Representations of the *banlieue*, like those of the *beurs*, are thus not to be understood in terms of transparent representations of reality, but as discursive constructs and sites of struggle for meaning" (*Reframing* 18).

4. The French system of *intégration* in many ways has been modeled on the expectation that immigrants and their children will simply assimilate into mainstream France. Of course, a good deal of research demonstrates that the second and third generation children of immigrants, who constituted many of the rioters, have assimilated into French society. On this process of assimilation, see Michèle Tribalat, *De l'immigration à l'assimilation*.

5. In his analysis of space in *La Haine*, Adrian Fielder has pointed out that the *cité* represents a grid that regulates, interpellates, and controls individuals. Fielder claims that the spatial intrigue of films like *La Haine* resides in the individual's struggle to subvert this mapping process (270). In many ways the riots can be understood as a similar spatial struggle.

6. Sylvie Durmelat argues that the media's representations of the *banlieue* have opposed "center to periphery, cleanliness to filth, civilized to savage, native to foreign, and historical heritage to disquieting modernity" (181).

7. On the denial of discrimination in French politics by both leftist and

rightist constituencies and the relationship to policies of *intégration*, see Erick Bleich's *Race Politics in Britain and France*.

8. Theorists and commentators from diverse backgrounds seemed to all concur in one way or another that the riots were caused by a clash of Islam and the West. Frequently, their comments emanated from stereotypes of Arabs as macho and of French youths of North African heritage as directionless thrill seekers as evidenced in Foued Ajami's "The Boys of Nowhere" and Alain Finkielkraut's interview in *Ha'aretz*.

9. Daniel Pipes in "Reflections of the Revolution in France" and Charles Krautheimer in "What the Uprising Wants" were two examples of commentators in the United States who made this claim.

10. The incorporation of these images brings to mind the posed style of the images included in Alloula's *Le Harem colonial*, discussed in the introduction. In many ways the images in *Indigènes*, intended as they seem to be on unmasking the colonial gaze and recognizing the agency of the North African soldiers, function much as they were intended to function in Alloula's project.

11. This work represents one of the most recent and comprehensive attempts in France to address the colonial heritage from a variety of different perspectives in an edited volume with multiple contributors. Other important studies similar to this include, among others, Pascal Blanchard's *Culture coloniale*, written with Sandrine Lemaire, and the many works by Marc Ferro and Benjamin Stora, such as, respectively, *Histoire des colonisations* and *La Gangrène et l'oubli*.

12. Pierre Nora's conceptualization of the *lieu de mémoire* has been criticized of this very focus on the nation to the exclusion of an understanding of the underpinnings of the nation's composition. See, for instance, Emily Apter's *Continental Drift* (1–6).

13. The concept of multidirectional memory, according to Michael Rothberg, functions to decolonize the memory of historical episodes. Rothberg argues that the memories of the Holocaust and memories of colonization and genocide need not be exclusive, as they are frequently portrayed to be (160–70).

14. On the relationship of France to its colonial histories, see Robert Aldrich's "Colonial Past, Post-Colonial Present" and "Coming to Terms with the Colonial Past."

3. HIDDEN MAPS OF VICTIMIZATION

1. See, for instance, the special seven-page commemorative issue on Algeria in *Le Monde*, "Algérie: 1962–2002." In Algeria this focus on the nation's experience of colonial history is best discerned in the state's creation of mythical

heroes and martyrs of the independence movement. As one unnamed Algerian contributor to the commemorative issue remarked, "On a crée des héros et des mythes, et qu'est-ce que ça a donné? Une tromperie" (They created heroes and myths and to what did that lead? Fraud) (13).

2. Mireille Rosello points out that current Franco-Algerian relations, for instance, are marked by the absence of a "rencontre," or meeting point, and that this fracture emanates from the Algerian War: "Dans la mémoire contemporaine des deux pays, la fracture que constitute la guerre de libération sert souvent de point d'origine" (In the contemporary memory of both countries, the fracture that constitutes the war of liberation often serves as an originary point) (França 788). I agree with Rosello but would suggest that the "volonté de rencontre," or desire to meet, that she identifies as missing in the countries' relations is nonetheless frequently present in the proliferation of diverse memories of the colonial period. However, it is the ability to relate that is ultimately vitiated by the haunting and obsessive memories of the colonial period that quickly turn to memories of national culpability in France or national victimization in Algeria. The pervasive focus on the colonial period and its temporality that I am outlining here supports Ella Shohat's important observation that "the postcolonial implies a narrative of progression in which colonialism remains the central point of reference" (133). Shohat's understanding of the role of colonial temporality as a central organizing feature of the postcolonial can be seen in the form of postcolonial memory, which I examine here. With regard to postcolonial cinema, this temporality manifests itself in the focus and fetishization of images of colonial victimization. Set within the postcolonial context, many films, such as *Caché*, demonstrate an obsessive return within the narrative to the temporal context of colonialism.

3. On drawing and its relationship to trauma in the film, see Austin Guy's article "Drawing Trauma."

4. Paul Gilroy takes the film to task for not engaging sufficiently with the historical dimensions of colonial history and with 1961 France: "Many people involved in building a habitable multicultural Europe will feel that there are pressing issues of morality and responsibility involved in raising that history only to reduce it to nothing more than a piece of tragic machinery in the fatal antagonism that undoes *Caché*'s protagonists. The dead deserve better than that passing acknowledgement" (233). Gilroy's reading seems to overlook how the film builds the insistence of colonial history as a haunting and repeatable structure into its representation. In many ways the film reflects that France's

colonial history is ever present yet never fully addressed, thus underscoring the very problem that Gilroy identifies in it.

5. This awareness corresponded to the vote of the Assemblée Nationale in 1999 to recognize the Algerian War as such rather than as the "événements," or events, of 1954–62. Shortly thereafter the Algerian President Abdelaziz Bouteflika made the first visit to France by an Algerian President since 1983.

6. These publications were complemented by the recent passing of 2003, the year of Algeria (*l'année de l'Algérie en France*), which witnessed a series of events commemorating France's relationship to Algeria.

7. Bertrand Benoit's book *Le Syndrome algérien* also treats the French obsession with a phantasmatic Algeria. Although its focus is the establishment of French politics on Algeria in relationship to contradictory beliefs and fantasies, it too is concerned with the way Algeria holds such importance in the French imaginary.

8. Of course even when attention is focused on the contemporary plight of Maghrebians in France, the focal point frequently returns us either back to the colonial era or to retrospective visions of ethnic affiliation that seem to come straight out of that period. Media coverage of the recent and provocative debate on secularism in France concerning the right to signify religious affiliation in school often features diverse perspectives of Islamic women, but nearly always focuses on Islam and its visible signifiers as a contentious point of cultural identification. Such perspectives implicitly reference colonial-era images and attitudes regarding Islam as a disruptive difference.

9. Michel Foucault illustrates how the dead are ultimately subject to a national surveillance. Assimilated into the pedagogical archive of the nation and known through the gaze of medical examination, the dead contribute to the nation and are continuously at its service, according to Foucault (146). In a similar manner the dead bodies of colonial history to which I am calling attention here are also implicated in surveillance by the nationalist gaze, albeit one whose intention is to undermine the nationalist ideals of the past. Yet, the archival and pedagogical nature attributed to the colonial dead suggests their service and incorporation within nationalist discourses nonetheless. Such an appropriation, I maintain, remains a problematic point of identification that often only consolidates enclosed notions of national heritage.

10. For other texts treating the colonial era in Algeria from a similar perspective, see Paul Aussaresses; Jean Debernard; Jacques Duquesne; Jean Faure; Monique Hervo; Michel Roux; Marie-Pierre Ulloa.

11. See chapter 4 for a full discussion of Azouz Begag's work.

12. On the role of the immobile camera and the way it reappears at the end of the film, see D. I. Grossvogel's article "Haneke." Grossvogel argues that the tale of race and a Brechtian distancing seen in the camera work of the film build a meta-critical perspective into the filmic narrative that forces the spectator to reflect upon questions ultimately posed by the film. Although Grossvogel does not discuss victimization in relation to Brechtian distancing, his argument on the film's formal qualities can be seen to align with my discussion of the way the film builds the question of the haunting temporality of colonial victimization into its form.

13. On the role of the gaze in relationship to terror, see Elizabeth Ezra and Jane Sillars. Although they don't focus on victimization, their analysis of the film's emphasis on watching and waiting as a form of terror can also be seen as terror in relationship to postcolonial victimization: "In a world where turning a blind eye has become an art, Michael Haneke's 2005 *Caché/Hidden* explores the ways in which being made to look — and to think — can be experienced as forms of terror" (215).

14. This brings to mind Charles de Gaulle's famous expression "L'Algérie française," or French Algeria. However, in the postcolonial era, the evolved version of this union has proven to be equally as difficult as it proved to be during de Gaulle's term of leadership during the colonial era.

15. Compare this to the recent blockbuster film *Michou d'Auber*, starring Gerard Depardieu. With an ailing mother and a father who cannot take care of him, Messaoud, a nine-year-old boy from Algeria living in Aubervilliers, is adopted by a French family living in the village of Berry and given the name Michel. The year is 1960, at the height of the Algerian War, and in contrast to the related terrorism taking place in Algeria and France, Messaoud is able to live a fairly stable life with his new family. However, much like the history of adoption in *Caché*, the story of adoption in *Michou d'Auber* is set in the French country village, where adoption places him through the suppression of Algerian identity, suggesting the depth of national roots in relationship to the quintessential image of the French family.

16. On this incident, see the recent work by Alain Dewerpe.

17. On the terrorism that is ravaging contemporary Algeria today in this form, see Hugh Roberts; Benjamin Stora, *Algeria, 1830–2000*; William B. Quandt; and Martin Stone.

18. For Max Silverman the film represents the possibility for shifting the postcolonial paradigm toward dialogue: "*Caché* offers some hope that the infernal circle of the colonial paradigm may be broken by the dialogue and

shifting perspectives of a postcolonial paradigm" (249). Contrary to Silverman, I believe the film underscores the difficult shift of the postcolonial paradigm when colonial history and an accompanying reciprocal victimization remain central to it.

4. CREATING AN OLD MAGHREB

1. The term *beur* was invented in the early 1980s by children of North African heritage in France. It was created to protest this group's treatment by the white French majority but has proved to be a problematic label. As Tarr puts it, "While it originally expressed an awareness of and refusal to be trapped by the negative meanings of the word 'Arab' in the French imaginary (which conflates differences between Algerians, Moroccans and Tunisians, Arabs and Berbers, first-generation immigrants and their French-born children and grandchildren), its subsequent patronizing, ghettoizing appropriation by dominant discourses, notably in the media, quickly became unacceptable to many of those to whom it referred. A self-designated slang variant, 'les rebeus,' has developed in the *banlieue*, but while many now refer to themselves as being of Maghrebi (or more specifically Algerian, Moroccan, or Tunisian) descent, some choose rather to identify themselves as Maghrebis in France, while others prefer not to acknowledge the Maghrebi aspect of their bicultural heritage" ("Maghrebi-French" 31). The difficulties of naming this segment of the population indicate, as Tarr suggests, its problematic status in relationship to French culture. For a more involved discussion of the use of the term *beur* and its political contestations, see Alec Hargreaves and Mark McKinney.

2. Although Tarr notes that the term can be potentially reductive, she defines *cinema de banlieu* as "a way of categorizing a series of independently released films set in the rundown multi-ethnic working-class estates (the *cités*) on the periphery of France's major cities (the *banlieues*)" (*Reframing* 15).

3. In a recent "remapping" of *beur* cinema in the new millennium, Allison Murray Levine argues that the representations of spatial boundaries and borders in *beur* films have become more porous and permeable: "I argue for an aesthetic and thematic shift in recent Beur cinema toward the portrayal of borders as permeable boundaries and of formerly excluded spaces such as the banlieues as sites of dynamic cultural exchange. Furthermore, it is my contention that this shift recognizes and reflects the position of Beur cinema within French cinema: rather than a minority cinema responding to a majority discourse, it is both inside and outside French cinema, a force for critique from without but also for change from within" (42). Even if the representation of such

spatial borders suggests porosity, that portrayal often plays itself off against the representation of Algeria as a space frozen in a colonial-era temporality.

4. The use of the colonial-era site and culture as a temporally lagged reference suggests Bhabha's conception of the "time-lag," whereby colonial culture comes back to revise modernity. However, in the films I examine here, Algeria as a time-lagged representation suggests the colonial past as an archival and static, rather than dynamic, location of culture. See Bhabha's *The Location of Culture*.

5. I do not mean to suggest that *beur* films do not treat the difficult integration of their characters into France and all of the accompanying issues of contact between cultures that entails. However, I am referring more to those aspects of *beur* cinema that portray characters, generally the parents or siblings who are unable to integrate fully into French culture, as inhabiting a distinct sphere, one that is more removed from France than that inhabited by the integrating protagonist.

6. On the question of *beur* cinema as an oppositional or resistant form related to identity politics, see Peter Bloom; Abbas Fahdel; and Christian Bosséno.

7. Much has been written on the hybrid and ironic representations of social space in *beur* cinema and literature. Without a doubt, representations of the *beur* protagonist's experience of social space frequently do exhibit these qualities. However, my interest is in the ways these films play that experience off against more binary representations of social space, coded in an East-West opposition. On the use of irony in *beur* texts, see Martine Delvaux.

8. On the representation of the patriarchal figure in the *beur* corpus, see Alec Hargreaves, "Resuscitating the Father."

9. Here, I am referring to Fanon's conception of the psychologically damned colonized figure in *Les damnés de la terre*.

10. On the issue of *beur* female identity in *Samia*, see Tarr's "Grrrls in the banlieu."

11. On Yamina Benguigui's *Mémoire's d'immigrés*, see Angelica Fenner; Kenneth Harrow; and Mark Ingram.

12. In *France and the Maghreb* Rosello identifies a dynamic, performative meeting point between the past and the present, Algeria and France.

13. The term "contact zone" originates from Mary Louise Pratt. Pratt defines contact zones as social spaces where cultures often grapple with one another while simultaneously being characterized by highly asymmetrical relations of power.

14. This is taken from Allouache's director's statement: July 2008, http://www.planet-dz.com/_En-Cours/SEPTEMBRE/allouache-merzak-lautre-monde.htm.

15. *Sambizanga* is a film about black resistance in Africa. Set just before the 1961 uprising against the Portuguese colonialists, the film, like *L'Autre monde*, centers on a young woman's search for her jailed husband. *Mortu Nega* tracks the role of women in the struggle for independence in Guinea-Bissau. The story's focus on the heroine Diminga and her loyalty to her husband, Sako, a wounded guerilla commander, establishes resonances with Allouache's film.

16. Taking Stora's comments further, we might surmise that the opaqueness of contemporary Algeria engenders the type of representational (re)turn to an "old Algeria" that I have outlined in this book. With the difficulties of representing contemporary Algeria, the emergence of a colonial-era Algeria within the contemporary context takes on more significance.

17. The phrase "apocalyptic tone" derives from Jacques Derrida. According to Derrida, the apocalyptic tone reveals the truth, whatever that truth might be. Interestingly, Derrida claims that the tone is analogous to an "unveiling in process" in that it reveals the truth or the end ("Apocalyptic" 83). Derrida's discussion of unveiling and the dynamics of the apocalyptic end resonate with Yasmine's experience in and of Algeria, particularly given the way her body remains trapped within the confines of a masculinist history of violence.

18. On the Algerian Syndrome, see the discussion of *Caché* in chapter 3. See also Anne Donadey.

5. COLONIAL CINEMA

1. In great part the crisis in Algerian identity can be traced to the politicization of language. Under French rule Arabic was suppressed, and by 1962 all the Algerian elites were French speaking. Between 1965 and 1978 President Boumedienne attempted to Arabize education. In 1979 there were demonstrations over the lack of jobs for Arab speakers, and French speakers were characterized as *Hizbal Franca* (the Party of France). The Berber population, comprising 15 to 20 percent of Algerians, clung to the French language as a means of resisting Arabization. Since 1988 the language dispute has become implicated in the controversy between secularists and Islamists, and the Islamist linkage of Arabic with Islam has denied Berbers a role in Algeria's future. The Front of Socialist Forces (FFS) has also been linked to *Hizbal Franca* and, like the Berbers, is threatened with marginalization in an Islamic state. An Islamic Arabic Algerian nation appeals to large numbers of Algerians in much the same way that the FLN, with its secular nationalism, appealed to a significant proportion of the populace at an earlier stage.

2. The result has been civil war, a domestic insurgency that has witnessed the death of at least fifty thousand Algerians since 1992, and a rapidly internationalizing conflict that has prompted the flight of nearly forty thousand productive, middle-class Algerians to France.

3. Since 1992 a large number of armed terrorists, factions, and splinter groups have emerged. All of these groups define themselves as "Islamic groups"; however, their leadership, composition, and aims are unclear in most instances. There are frequent reports of the formation of new groups, usually described as factions of existing groups. The main groups are the Armée islamique du salut (AIS), or the Islamic Salvation Army — the armed wing of the FIS, a group that claims to attack only security forces and military targets; and the Groupe islamique armé (GIA), or the Armed Islamic Group — an assembly of loosely organized groups whose leadership and composition remain unclear and who are reported to be responsible for killing numerous civilians, carrying out massacres, and committing other atrocities. The GIA has also issued death threats against FIS leaders and has reportedly killed FIS members and supporters. Other, reportedly small, armed groups who have also issued declarations include the Ligue islamique de la daawa et le djihad (LIDD), or the Islamic League for Preaching and Holy War, and the Front islamique pour le Djihad armé (FIDA), or the Islamic Front for Armed Holy War.

4. Michael Taussig writes of the "space of death," where death functions as a colonizing presence (50–65).

5. This scene refers to the manipulation of memory by Algeria in its representation of the FLN as uncontested victims and heroes. In a 2002 interview in *Le Monde* Stora spoke of this problem in Algeria and noted that Algeria "doit perdre le monopole de la mémoire, pour revenir à la société" (must lose the monopoly on memory in order to return to society) (20). The creation of the hero of national liberation depends on the idea of the nation as victim.

6. It is important to note that the novel rehearses the film's poetic realist themes of nostalgia and longing for one's "homeland." Berkane, much like Pépé, dreams of a return to an idealized homeland. Interestingly, both the France of Julien Duvivier's 1930s film and the Algeria of Assia Djebar's postcolonial novel are places marked by great social turmoil. The economic crisis of the 1930s interwar period situates Duvivier's France as a context to which Pépé cannot return, and fundamentalist violence and civil unrest characterize the context for Berkane's impossible return as well.

7. On this, see Henry Garrity.

8. Thus, Djebar emphasizes how colonialism's aesthetic forms condition the postcolonial subject and the collective memory of the postcolony. Here, colonial esthetics imprison, since they engender nostalgia and a nationalist desire, the illusion of taking root in a space which belongs to a delimited group, hence Berkane's "chez nous" (15).

9. The nostalgia associated with the photograph and the desire of an image ever more faded serves symbolically to anticipate death, according to Roland Barthes. For Barthes the photographic image reveals this death simultaneously future and anterior: "Je lis en même temps, *cela sera* et *cela a été*; j'observe avec horreur un futur antérieur dont la mort est l'enjeu" (I read at the same time: This will be and this has been; I observe with horror an anterior future of which death is the stake) (150).

10. Here, it is interesting to note that Berkane, like Pépé, is involved in with two women, representing his affiliation with both France and Algeria. Djebar mirrors Duvivier's love triangle of Inès, Gabby, and Pépé with Nadjia, Marise, and Berkane. This similarity further consolidates the equation I see established between Duvivier's colonial-era film and Djebar's postcolonial novel. Moreover, both "homelands" for the male protagonists are coded as an unattainable feminine. The closing sequence of shot/reverse shots in Duvivier's film between Gabby leaving for France and Pépé dying behind the port's iron gates demonstrates the unattainable nature of France as a feminine ideal. In a similar manner Berkane's inability to rejoin the maternally coded Algeria parallels Duvivier's film.

11. This iterative desire to appropriate the woman's image as a strategic means of territorial control of Algeria is best underscored by Woodhull: "The cultural record makes clear that women embody Algeria not only for Algerians in the days since independence, but also for the French colonizers . . . In the colonialist fantasy, to possess Algeria's women is to possess Algeria" (16).

12. The sea as a maternal presence was first elaborated by Gaston Bachelard. The sea, argued Bachelard, often served the poetic imagination with maternal images, images linked to home and territory. It is not surprising that Berkane's problematic return is filtered through the conflation of the sea and the mother since he is most concerned with finding his authentic version of territory. This quest, as the novel will demonstrate, remains a futile and dangerous one that is trapped in the ideological paradigm of colonial victimization.

13. "Nedjma" recalls the colonial-era novel of Algerian independence by the same name written by Kateb Yacine.

14. I am inventing this term that seems particularly appropriate, given that the problematic of Berkane's interpretation of the Casbah is central to the novel. The novel functions as a labyrinth even as it attempts to deconstruct the mythology of hero and victim associated with this structure.

15. Rosello notes that the Casbah in Fanon's *Les damnés de la terre* is the structure for the colonial division of urban space that is "separated from itself by the colonial system" (*Postcolonial* 163). In a similar manner the Casbah in Djebar's *La Disparition de la langue française* shows how the contemporary division of Algerians is closely tied to the troubling memories of colonial culture that separates Algerian space and people from the present. It is as if postcolonial Algeria were divided by the same Manichean, colonial structure that occupies the Casbah as postcolonial memory place.

16. Speaking of civil violence in Algeria in 1988, Djebar articulates her remorse and her sense that Algerian culture is haunted by this past that refuses to let go: "Car je suis hantée pour ma part — et ce même avant cet orage — par un long et durable état de morbidité dans lequel s'est retrouvée la culture algérienne au présent [. . .] J'ai paru m'attarder sur les ruines d'un savoir déliquescent, don't l'échec pathétique aurait dû nous annoncer beaucoup plus tôt le prodromes d'une explosion: celle d'octobre 1988" (For I am myself haunted — and this, even before this storm — by a long and lasting state of morbidity in which Algerian culture presently finds itself [. . .] I seemed to linger on the ruins of a declining knowledge, whose pathetic failure should have at least announced to us much earlier the warning signs of an explosion: that of October 1988) (*Voix* 120).

17. In this sense *La Disparition* repeats the theme of suspension and of the specter seen in Djebar's *La Femme sans sépulture*, where the spectral voice of Zoulikha, heroine of the resistance, narrates her own experience of torture.

18. On the way terrorist cells are motivated by a territorialist desire rather than by religious adherence, see Robert Pape's controversial and popular book *Dying to Win*.

19. The title of the novel refers ironically to the exile of the Arabic language for more than one hundred years. This other "disappearance" shows the extent to which language in Djebar is implicit in the memory and the loss that condition vengeance and victimization. This implicit reference to the disappearance of the Arabic language uncovers the Manichean colonial dynamic that continues to structure culture in Algeria. Thus, Djebar denounces the influence of a singular cultural logic in Algeria.

CONCLUSION

1. In Camus's short story, Janine views the Algerian desert in the form of an enigmatic question mark at one point. The setting ultimately serves as the background for an existential crisis the couple, not unlike Richard and Susan in *Babel*, is experiencing. For more on the relationship between Camus and the nexus of colonialism and terrorism, see David Carroll's *Albert Camus the Algerian*.

2. The hill from which the boys shoot the rifle is similar to the tower of Babel, in that in climbing it the boys set in motion much confusion and division within an international community.

3. Moreover, Janine and Marcel represent this Western perspective in Camus's work, in that they cast their gaze at the Arabs in the bus and at the landscape they pass, understanding them as an opaque mirror from which their own colonial attitudes are reflected.

4. The photographic image contains an excess or haunting presence for Barthes that emerges within the force field of the photo, or what he refers to as the *studium*. The photograph captures something that is irretrievably lost and that enables the viewer to grasp a presence that cannot be subsumed into an existing paradigm (26). In *Babel* the wounding shot functions to relay the history of victimization and colonial attitudes that haunt the contemporary context and ultimately inform the ensuing announcements of terror.

5. In many ways the shot that penetrates the glass of the tourist bus in *Babel* can be understood as symbolic of the ways that terrorism penetrates the "glass eye," or the media camera. The "local" event slowly becomes magnified and disseminated as an act of terror within the larger international community.

6. *Terror's Advocate* won the 2008 César for Best Documentary and was nominated for Outstanding Directorial Achievement in Directing.

7. Schroeder's documentary plants the suggestion that Vergès himself, son of a Vietnamese mother and a member of the colonial student association during his university years, operated as a terrorist. Vergès's full biography still remains a mystery. He disappeared between 1970 and 1978, during which time, it is suggested in the documentary, he joined Pol Pot in Cambodia and acted as a secret agent for the French government. Schroeder's investigation reveals Vergès's involvement with Congolese dictator Moïse Tschombé. Vergès's prolonged absence also happens to coincide with the emergence of Waddi Haddad's international terrorist network, financed in part by a former Swiss Nazi, François Genoux, who supported the National Liberation Front in Algeria and Palestinian resistance movements, and is a close acquaintance of Vergès. Additionally, Vergès offered to represent Sadaam Hussein in his trial.

8. Thomas Gilou adapted the life story of his friend and screenwriter Messaoud Hattou, who lived through a similar experience as an adopted child.

9. The expression "time out of joint" is a reference to Shakespeare's *Hamlet* that Derrida employs in *Specters of Marx*. For Derrida a haunting remainder of history insists to demand justice. Recently, in *Algeria Cuts*, Khanna has characterized this insistence of the return of colonial history as a salutary gesture. I caution against the return of colonial history in the age of terror when its demands for justice focus on victimization.

Works Cited

Agamben, Giorgio. *Homo Sacer: Sovereign Power and Bare Life*. Stanford: Stanford University Press, 1998.

Ajami, Foued. "The Boys of Nowhere." *US News and World Report* 13 November 2005. 21 November 2005. http://www.usnews.com.

Aldrich, Robert. "Colonial Past, Post-Colonial Present: History Wars French Style." *History Australia* 3.1 (June 2006): 141–49.

———. "Coming to Terms with the Colonial Past: The French and Others." *Arts: The Journal of the Sydney University Arts Association* 28 (2006): 91–116.

Alleg, Henri. *La question*. Paris: Minuit, 1958.

Allouache, Merzak. "L'Autre Monde/The Other World." Director's Statement. Trans. Michael Dembrow. http://www.spot.pcc.edu/~mdembrow/otherworlddirectorsstatement.html.

Alloula, Malek. *The Colonial Harem*. Trans. Myrna Godzich and Wald Godzich. Minneapolis: University of Minneapolis Press, 1986.

Anderson, Benedict. *Imagined Communities: Reflections on the Origin and Spread of Nationalism*. London: Verso, 2006.

Apter, Emily. *Continental Drift: From National Characters to Virtual Subjects*. Chicago: University of Chicago Press, 1999.

Armes, Roy. *Postcolonial Images: Studies in North African Film*. Bloomington: Indiana University Press, 2006.

Aussaresses, Paul. *Services spéciaux, Algérie 1955–1957*. Paris: Perrin, 2001.

Bachelard, Gaston. *L'Eau et les rêves. Essais sur l'imagination de la matière*. Paris: J. Corti, 1942.

Bal, Mieke. "The Politics of Citation." *Diacritics* 21 (1991): 35–45.

Balibar, Etienne. *Les frontières de la démocratie*. Paris: La Découverte, 1992.

Balibar, Etienne, and Immanuel Wallerstein. *Race, Nation, Class: Ambiguous Identities*. Trans. Chris Turner. London: Verso, 1991.

Barthes, Roland. *Camera Lucida*. New York: Hill & Wang, 1981.

Bazin, André. *What is Cinema?* Berkeley: University of California Press, 1967.

Behdad, Ali. "Une Pratique Sauvage: Postcolonial Belatedness and Cultural Politics." *The Pre-Occupation of Postcolonial Studies*. Ed. Fawzia Afzal-Khan and Kalpana Seshadri-Crooks. Durham: Duke University Press, 2000. 71–85.

Benoit, Bertrand. *Le Syndrome algérien: L'imaginaire de la politique algérienne de la France*. Paris: L'Harmattan, 1995.

Betts, Gregory. "Wanted Women, Woman's Wants: *The Colonial Harem* and Postcolonial Discourse." *Canadian Review of Comparative Literature/Revue Canadienne de Littérature comparée* (September 1995): 257–549.

Bhabha, Homi. *The Location of Culture*. New York: Routledge, 1994.

———. "The World and the Home." *Dangerous Liaisons: Gender, Nation, & Postcolonial Perspectives*. Ed. Anne McClintock, Aamir Mufti, and Ella Shohat. Minneapolis: University of Minnesota Press, 1997. 445–55.

Blanchard, Pascal, Nicolas Bancel, and Sandrine Lemire. *La Fracture Coloniale:La société française au prisme de l'héritage colonial*. Paris: La Découverte, 2005.

Bleich, Erick. *Race Politics in Britain and France: Ideas and Policymaking since the 1960s*. Cambridge: Cambridge University Press, 2003.

Bloom, Peter. "Beur Cinema and the Politics of Location: French Immigration Politics and the Naming of a Film Movement." *Social Identities* 5.4 (1999): 469–87.

Bosséno, Christian. "Un Cinéma De Transition?" *CinemAction* 56 (1990): 146–47.

Bouchareb, Rachid. "Debt of Honor." *Time* 28 October 2006. November 2006. http://www.time.com/time/europe/eu/article/.hmtl.

Branche, Raphael. *La Torture et l'armée pendant la guerre d'Algérie*. Paris: Gallimard, 2001.

Camus, Albert. *Exile and the Kingdom*. Trans. Carol Cosman. New York: Vintage, 2007.

Carroll, David. *Albert Camus the Algerian: Colonialism, Terror, Justice*. New York: Columbia University Press, 2007.

Celli, Carlo. *Gillo Pontecorvo: From Resistance to Terrorism*. Lantham: Scarecrow Press, 2005.

Chakrabarty, Dipesh. *Provincializing Europe: Postcolonial Thought and Historical Difference*. Princeton: Princeton University Press, 2007.

Chambers, Iain. *Culture after Humanism: History, Culture, Subjectivity*. London: Routledge, 2001.

———. *Mediterranean Crossings: The Politics of an Interrupted Modernity*. Durham: Duke University Press, 2008.

Chanan, Michael. "The Changing Geography of Third Cinema." *Screen* 38.4 (Winter 1997).

——. "Outsiders: *The Battle of Algiers* and Political Cinema." *Sight and Sound* 9 (2007): 38–40.

Chanda, Nayan, and Strobe Talbott. *The Age of Terror: America and the World after September 11*. New York: Basic Books, 2001.

Chow, Rey. *The Age of the World Target: Self-Referentiality in War, Theory, and Comparative Work*. Durham: Duke University Press, 2006.

Conley, Tom. *Cartographic Cinema*. Minneapolis: University of Minnesota Press, 2007.

Dawson, Jan. *Monthly Film Bulletin* January 1971.

Debernard, Jean. *Simples Soldats*. Paris: Actes Sud, 2001.

Deleuze, Gilles, and Félix Guattari. *Anti-Oedipus: Capitalism and Schizophrenia*. Trans. Robert Hurley, Helen Lane, and Mark Seem. Minneapolis: University of Minnesota Press, 1983.

——. *Mille Plateaux. Capitalisme et schizophrénie II*. Paris: Minuit, 1980.

Delvaux, Martine. "L'ironie du sort: Le tiers espace dans la littérature beure." *The French Review* 68.4 (1995): 681–93.

Derrida, Jacques. *L'écriture et la différence*. Paris: Seuil, 1979.

——. "Of an Apocalyptic Tone Recently Adopted in Philosophy," *Semeia* 23 (1982): 63–97.

——. *Specters of Marx: The State of Debt, the Work of Mourning, and the New International*. Trans. Peggy Kamuf. New York: Routledge, 1994.

Dewerpe, Alain. *Charonne, 8 février 1962, anthropologie historique d'un massacre d'Etat*. Paris: Gallimard, 2006.

Diawara, Manthia. *African Cinema: Politics and Culture*. Bloomington: Indiana University Press, 1992.

Djebar, Assia. *Ces voix qui m'assiègent: En marge de ma francophonie*. Paris: Albin Michel, 1999.

——. *La Disparition de la langue française*. Paris: Albin Michel, 2003.

——. *La femme sans sépulture*. Paris: Albin Michel, 2002.

Donadey, Anne. "'Une Certaine Idée de la France': The Algeria Syndrome and Struggles over French Identity." *Identity Papers: Contested Nationhood in Twentieth-Century France*. Ed. Steven Ungar and Tom Conley. Minneapolis: University of Minnesota Press, 1996. 215–32.

Downing, John. "Post Tri-Color African Cinema." *Cinema, Colonialism, Postcolonialism: Perspectives from the French and Francophone World*. Ed. Dina Sherzer. Austin: University of Texas Press, 1996.

Duquesne, Jacques. *Pour comprendre la guerre d'Algérie*. Paris: Plon, 2001.

Durmelat, Sylvie. "On Natives and Narratives from the Banlieues." *Women, Immigration and Identities in France*. Ed. J. Freeman and C. Tarr. Oxford: Berg, 2001. 171–88.

Ebert, Roger. "The Battle of Algiers." 30 May 1968. June 2007. http://www.rogerebert.com.

Einaudi, Jean-Luc, and Maurice Rajsfus. *Les silences de la police 16 juillet 1942, 17 octobre 1961*. Paris: L'Esprit Frapperu, 2001.

Erdem, Engin. "The Clash of Civilizations: Revisited after September 11." *Alternatives* 1.2 (2002).

Ezra, Elizabeth. *The Colonial Unconscious: Race and Culture in Interwar France*. New York: Cornell University Press, 2000.

———. *European Cinema*. Oxford: Oxford University Press, 2004.

Ezra, Elizabeth, and Jane Sillars. "Hidden in Plain Sight: Bringing Terror Home." *Screen* 48.2 (Summer 2007): 215–21.

Fahdel, Abbas. "Une esthétique Beur?" *CinemAction* 56 (1990): 140–51.

Fanon, Frantz. *Black Skin, White Masks*. New York: Grove Press, 2008.

———. *A Dying Colonialism*. Trans. H. Chevalier. New York: Grove Press, 1965.

———. *Les damnés de la terre*. Paris: Maspero, 1961.

Faure, Jean. *Au pays de la soif et de la peur*. Paris: Flammarion, 2001.

Fenner, Angelica. "Aural Topographies of Migration in Yamina Benguigui's Inch'Allah Dimanche." *Camera Obscura: A Journal of Feminism, Culture, and Media Studies* 22.3,66 (2007): 93–127.

Ferro, Marc. *Histoire des colonisations: Des conquëtes aux indépendances, XIIe–XXe siècle*. Paris: Seuil, 1994.

Fielder, Adrian. "Poaching on Public Space: Urban Autonomous Zones in French Banlieue Films." *Film and Urban Societies in a Global Context*. Ed. M. Shiel and T. Fitzmaurice. Oxford: Blackwell, 2001. 270–81.

Finkielkraut, Alain. Interview. *Ha'aretz* 21 November 2005. December 2006. http://www.haaretz.com.

Foucault, Michel. *The Birth of the Clinic: An Archaeology of Medical Perception*. Trans. A. M. Sheridan Smith. New York: Vintage, 1973.

Freund, Charles Paul. "The Pentagon's Film Festival: A Primer for *The Battle of Algiers*." *Reason* 27 December 2003. February 2005. http://www.reason.com.

Gabriel, Teshome. "Third Cinema as Guardian of Popular Memory: Towards a Third Aesthetics." *Questions of Third Cinema*. Ed. Jim Pines and Paul Willemen. London: BFI, 1994. 53–64.

———. *Third Cinema in the Third World: The Dynamics of Style and Liberation*. Michigan: UMI, 1979.

Garrity, Henry. "Narrative Space in Julien Duvivier's *Pépé le Moko*." *French Review* 65.4 (March 1992): 623–28.

Geesey, Patricia. "'Faites comme chez vous': Spatial and Cultural Appropriation in Franco-Maghrebi Cinema." *Discursive Geographies: Writing Space and Place in French/Géographies discursives: L'Ecriture de l'espace et du lieu en français*. Ed. Jeanne Garane. Amsterdam: Rodopi, 2005. 193–206.

Gilroy, Paul. *Postcolonial Melancholia*. New York: Columbia University Press, 2006.

Golsan, Richard. *The Papon Affair: Memory and Justice on Trial*. New York: Routledge, 2000.

Gourevitch, Philip. "Winning and Losing." *The New Yorker* 22 December 2003: 53.

Grossvogel, D. I. "Haneke: The Coercing of Vision." *Film Quarterly* 60.4 (2007): 36–43.

Guy, Austin. "Drawing Trauma: Visual Testimony in *Caché* and *J'ai 8 ans*." *Screen* 48.4 (Winter 2007): 529–36.

Hallward, Peter. *Absolutely Postcolonial: Writing between the Singular and the Specific*. Manchester: Manchester University Press, 2001.

Hardt, Michael, and Antonio Negri. *Empire*. Cambridge: Harvard University Press, 1999.

Hargreaves, Alec. "Resuscitating the Father: New Cinematic Representations of the Maghrebi Minority in France." *Sites* 4 (2000): 343–51.

Hargreaves, Alec, and Mark McKinney. *Post-Colonial Cultures in France*. London: Routledge, 1997.

Harrow, Kenneth. "Mémoires d'immigrés: Bougnoul for What?" *Postcolonial Theory and Francophone Literary Studies*. Ed. Anne Donadey and Adlai Murdoch. Gainesville: University Press of Florida, 2005. 102–25.

Hervo, Monique. *Chroniques du bidonville: Nanterre en guerre d'Algérie*. Paris: Seuil, 2001.

Higbee, Will. "Re-Presenting the Urban Periphery: Maghrebi-French Filmmaking and the Banlieue Film." *Cineaste: America's Leading Magazine on the Art and Politics of the Cinema* 33.1 (Winter 2007): 38–43.

Honeycutt, Kirk. "Days of Glory." *The Hollywood Reporter* 25 May 2006.

Huntington Samuel. *The Clash of Civilizations and the Remaking of the World Order*. New York: Simon & Schuster, 1998.

Ingram, Mark. "Voices Unveiled. Mémoires d'immigrés, L'Héritage maghrébin." *Moving Pictures, Migrating Identities*. Ed. Eva Rueschmann. Jackson: University Press of Mississippi, 2003. 105–20.

Iverem, Esther. "Samia: Calling All Black Girls." *SeeingBlack.com* 17 May 2001. April 2006. http://www.seeingblack.com/samia.

Jameson, Fredric. *Postmodernism or the Cultural Logic of Late Capitalism*. Durham: Duke University Press, 1991.

Kael, Pauline. "The Battle of Algiers." *The New Yorker* 15 January 1973.

Kaufman, Michael. "What Does the Pentagon See in Battle of Algiers?" *New York Times* 7 September 2003. December 2006. http://www.nytimes.com/2003/09/07/weekinreview/07/kauf.html.

Kédadouche, Zaïr. *La France et les beurs*. Paris: La Table Ronde, 2002.

Khanna, Ranjanna. *Algeria Cuts: Women and Representation, 1830 to the Present*. Stanford: Stanford University Press, 2007.

———. "Post-Palliative." *Postcolonial Text* 2.1 (2006). http://www.postcolonial.org.

Krautheimer, Charles. "What the Uprising Wants." *Time* 13 November 2005. May 2007. http://www.time.com/time/magazine.

Laroussi, Farid. "Literature in Migration." *The European Legacy* 7.6 (2002): 709–22.

Lazreg, Marnia. *The Eloquence of Silence: Algerian Women in Question*. London: Routledge, 1994.

Lemire, Laurent. "Des feux mal éteints." *Le Nouvel Observateur* May 2002: 22–23.

Levine, Allison Murray. "Mapping Beur Cinema in the New Millenium." *Journal of Film and Video* 60.3–4 (Fall–Winter 2008): 42–59.

Lewis, Bernard. "The Roots of Muslim Rage." *The Atlantic Monthly* September 1990: 47–60.

Mbembe, Achille. *On the Postcolony*. Berkeley: University of California Press, 2001.

Naficy, Hamid. *An Accented Cinema: Exilic and Diasporic Filmmaking*. Princeton: Princeton University Press, 2001.

Nora, Pierre. *Les Lieux de mémoire*. Paris: Gallimard, 1984.

Pape, Robert. *Dying to Win: The Strategic Logic of Suicide Terrorism*. New York: Random, 2005.

Pipes, Daniel. "Reflections on the Revolution in France." *New York Sun* 8 November 2005. December 2007. http://www.nysun.com/foreign/reflections-on-the-revolution-in-france/22702.

Pratt, Mary Louise. "Arts of the Contact Zone." *Ways of Reading: An Anthology for Writers*. Ed. David Bartholomae and Anthony Petroski. 5th ed. Boston: Bedford-St. Martin's, 1999. 582–96.

Proyect, Louis. "Looking Back at *The Battle of Algiers*." *Monthly Review* 8 December 2005. January 2007. http://www.mrzine.monthlyreview.org.proyect120805.html.

Quandt, William B. *Between Ballots and Bullets: Algeria's Transition from Authoritarianism*. London: Brookings, 1998.

Rainer, Peter. "Prescient Tense." *New York Magazine* 5 January 2004. http://www.nymag.com/nymetro/movies/revies/n_9697/.

Rey, Benoist. *Les Égorgeurs*. Paris: Minuit, 1961.

Reynolds, Paul. "Papers Show U.S. Torture Debates." BBC. 28 June 2004.

Rice-Sayre, Laura. "Veiled Threats: Malek Alloula's *Colonial Harem*." *Boundary 2: An International Journal of Literature and Culture* 15.1–2 (Fall 1986–Winter 1987): 351–63.

Roberts, Hugh. *The Battlefield: Algeria 1988–2000, Studies in a Broken Polity*. London: Verso, 2003.

Rondeau, Jean-Pierre. *Aspects véritables de la rebellion algérienne suivi de: Algérie médicale*. Paris: Dualpha, 2001.

Rosello, Mireille. *Declining the Stereotype: Ethnicity and Representation in French Cultures*. Hanover: University Press New England, 1998.

———. "França-Algéries ou Djazaïr-frances?" *Fractales et Mésententes fructueuses*. MLN 1.18 (4) (September 2003): 787–806.

———. *France and the Maghreb: Performative Encounters*. Gaineseville: University Press of Florida, 2005.

———. *Postcolonial Hospitality: The Immigrant as Guest*. Stanford: Stanford University Press, 2001.

Rothberg, Michael. "Between Auschwitz and Algeria: Multidirectional Memory and the Counterpublic Witness." *Critical Inquiry* 33.1 (Autumn 2006): 158–84.

Rousso, Henry. *Le Syndrome de Vichy*. Paris: Seuil, 1987.

Rousso, Henry, and Eric Conan. *Vichy, un passé qui ne passera pas*. Paris: Gallimard, 1996.

Roux, Michel. *Les Harkis: Les Oubliés de l'histoire, 1954–1991*. Paris: La Découverte, 1991.

Said, Edward. "The Clash of Ignorance." *The Nation* 22 October 2001. December 2007. http://www.thenation.com/doc/2011022/said.

———. *Culture and Imperialism*. New York: Knopf, 1993.

——. *Orientalism*. New York: Random, 1979.

Santner, Eric. *Stranded Objects: Mourning, Memory, and Film in Postwar Germany*. Ithaca: Cornell University Press, 1993.

Shohat, Ella. *Taboo Memories: Diasporic Voices*. Durham: Duke University Press, 2006.

Silverman, Max. "The Empire Looks Back." *Screen* 48.2 (Summer 2007): 245–49.

Silverstein, Paul, and Chantal Tetreault. "Postcolonial Urban Apartheid." *Riots in France* 11 June 2006. June 2007. http://riotsfrance.ssrc.org.

Smith, Craig. "Rioting Spreads in Paris Suburbs as Angry Youths Burn More Cars." *New York Times* 4 November 2005. June 2008. http://www.nytimes.com/2005/11/06/international/europe/06paris.

Solanas, Fernando, and Ocatvio Gettino. "Towards a Third Cinema." *Afterimage* 3 (1971): 16–35.

Spivak, Gayatri Chakravorty. *A Critique of Postcolonial Reason: Toward a History of the Vanishing Present*. Cambridge: Harvard University Press, 1999.

Spivak, Gayatri Chakravorty, and Sneja Gunew. "Questions of Multiculturalism." *The Cultural Studies Reader*. Ed. Simon During. London: Routledge, 1993. 193–202.

Stam, Robert, and Ella Shohat. *Multiculturalism, Postcoloniality, and Transnational Media*. New Brunswick: Rutgers University Press, 2008.

Stam, Robert, and Louis Spence. "Colonialism, Racism, and Representation." *Screen* 24.2 (March–April 1983): 2–20.

Stone, Martin. *The Agony of Algeria*. New York: Columbia University Press, 1997.

Stora, Benjamin. *Algeria, 1830–2000: A Short History*. Trans. Jane Marie Todd. Ithaca: Cornell University Press, 2004.

——. *La Gangrène et l'oubli: La mémoire de la guerre d'Algérie*. Paris: Découverte, 1998.

——. *La guerre invisible: Algérie, années 90*. Paris: Presses de Sciences Po, 2001.

——. "La mémoire retrouvée de la guerre d'Algérie." *Le Monde* 18 March 2002: 20–21.

Tanzer, Joshua. "Teen and Not Heard." *OffOffOff* 8 March 2001. January 2006. http://www.offoffoff.com/film/2001/samia.php.

Tarr, Carrie. "'Grrrls in the banlieu': Philippe Faucon's Samia and Fabrice Généstal's La Squale." *Esprit Créateur* 42.3 (Fall 2002): 28–38.

——. "Maghrebi-French (Beur) Filmmaking in Context." *Cineaste* 33.1 (Winter 2007): 2, 31–54.

——. "Questions of Identity in Beur Cinema: From *Tea in the Harem* to *Cheb*." *Screen* 34.4 (Winter 1993): 321–42.

——. *Reframing Difference: Beur and Banlieue Filmmaking in France*. New York: Manchester University Press, 2005.

Taussig, Michael T. *Shamanism, Colonialism, and the Wild Man: A Study in Terror and Healing*. Chicago: University of Chicago Press, 1992.

Temime, Emile. *France, Terre d'immigration*. Paris: Gallimard, 1999.

Thenault, Sylvie. *Une drôle de justice: Les magistrats dans la guerre d'Algérie*. Paris: Découverte, 2001.

Tribalat, Michèle. *De l'immigration à l'assimilation: Enquête sur les populations d'origine immigrée*. Paris: Découverte-INED, 1996.

Ulloa, Marie-Pierre. *Francis Jeanson, un intellectuel en dissidence, de la Résistance à la guerre d'Algérie*. London: Berg, 2001.

Vidal-Naquet, Pierre. *Les crimes de l'armée française: Algérie 1954–1962*. Paris: Découverte, 2001.

Wayne, Mike. *Political Cinema: The Dialectics of Third Cinema*. London: Pluto, 2001.

Weil, Patrick. *La République et sa diversité: Immigration, integration, et discrimination*. Paris: Seuil, 2005.

Woodhull, Winifred. *Transfigurations of the Maghreb: Feminism, Decolonization, and Literatures*. Minneapolis: University of Minnesota Press, 1993.

Yacine, Kateb. *Nedjma*. Paris: Seuil, 1956.

Young, Robert. *Colonial Desire: Hybridity in Theory, Culture, and Race*. London: Routledge, 1995.

——. *Postcolonialism: An Historical Introduction*. London: Blackwell, 2001.

FILMOGRAPHY

Allouache, Merzak. *L'Autre monde*. 2001.

Begag, Azuouz, and Christophe Ruggia. *Le Gone du Chaâba*. 1998.

Benguigui, Yamina. *Inch'Allah Dimanche*. 2001.

Bouchareb, Rachid. *Indigènes*. 2006.

Duvivier, Julien. *Pépé le Moko*. 1941.

Haneke, Michael. *Caché*. 2005.

Iñárritu, Alejandro González. *Babel*. 2006.

Nini, Soraya, and Philippe Faucon. *Samia*. 2000.

Pontecorvo, Gillo. *La battaglia di Algeri*. 1966.

Sembene, Ousmane. *Camp de Thiaroye*. 1987.

——. *Emitai*. 1971.

Index

In the France Overseas series

To Hell and Back
The Life of Samira Bellil
Samira Bellil
Translated by Lucy R. McNair
Introduction by Alec
G. Hargreaves

Colonial Metropolis
The Urban Grounds of
Anti-Imperialism and
Feminism in Interwar Paris
Jennifer Anne Boittin

The French Navy and
the Seven Years' War
Jonathan R. Dull

I, Nadia, Wife of a Terrorist
Baya Gacemi

Transnational Spaces and Identities
in the Francophone World
Edited by Hafid Gafaïti,
Patricia M. E. Lorcin, and
David G. Troyansky

French Colonialism Unmasked
The Vichy Years in
French West Africa
Ruth Ginio

Bourdieu in Algeria
Colonial Politics, Ethnographic
Practices, Theoretical Developments
Edited and with an introduction
by Jane E. Goodman and
Paul A. Silverstein

Endgame 1758
The Promise, the Glory, and the
Despair of Louisbourg's Last Decade
A. J. B. Johnston

Cinema in an Age of Terror
North Africa, Victimization,
and Colonial History
Michael F. O'Riley

Making the Voyageur World
Travelers and Traders in the
North American Fur Trade
Carolyn Podruchny

A Workman Is Worthy of His Meat
Food and Colonialism in Gabon
Jeremy Rich

The Moroccan Soul
French Education, Colonial
Ethnology, and Muslim
Resistance, 1912–1956
Spencer D. Segalla

Silence Is Death
The Life and Work of Tahar Djaout
Julija Šukys

Beyond Papillon
The French Overseas
Penal Colonies, 1854–1952
Stephen A. Toth

Madah-Sartre
The Kidnapping, Trial, and
Conver(sat/s)ion of Jean-Paul Sartre
and Simone de Beauvoir
Written and translated
by Alek Baylee Toumi
With an introduction by
James D. Le Sueur

To order or obtain more information on these or other University of Nebraska Press titles, visit www.nebraskapress.unl.edu.